The Real Tom Jones

To Dike,
Hope you enjoy the book!

Tom Jones

The Real Tom Jones

◆

Handicapped? Not Me

by Tom Jones

iUniverse, Inc.
New York Lincoln Shanghai

The Real Tom Jones
Handicapped? Not Me

All Rights Reserved © 2003 by Thomas L. Jones

No part of this book may be reproduced or transmitted in any form or by any means, graphic, electronic, or mechanical, including photocopying, recording, taping, or by any information storage retrieval system, without the written permission of the publisher.

iUniverse, Inc.

For information address:
iUniverse, Inc.
2021 Pine Lake Road, Suite 100
Lincoln, NE 68512
www.iuniverse.com

ISBN: 0-595-27166-9

Printed in the United States of America

I dedicate the story of my life to four individuals, without whose help I would never have had a life. My parents, Carl and Mary Lois Jones, made me realize that anything can be accomplished with hard work. Tim Nugent made sure higher education was available to me and many other persons with disabilities. And without Louise, the love-of-my-life partner to whom I have been married for 44 years, I would never have gained any measure of success.

Contents

Foreword... xi
Introduction... xv
CHAPTER 1   The Gun Wasn't Loaded........................ 1
CHAPTER 2   There is a Solution to Every Problem......... 5
CHAPTER 3   A Cardinal Fan in Cub Territory.............. 10
CHAPTER 4   A Career in Radio Beckons................... 13
CHAPTER 5   First College, Then Television............... 19
CHAPTER 6   The Love of My Life.......................... 24
CHAPTER 7   Wheelchair Safari Invades South Africa....... 30
CHAPTER 8   They Really Pay Me to do This?............... 37
CHAPTER 9   TV Sports Director on Wheels................. 45
CHAPTER 10   In Search of the Big Ones.................... 53
CHAPTER 11   Two More Jobs and Willie Nelson.............. 59
CHAPTER 12   Advice for the Medical Profession............ 68
CHAPTER 13   Negotiation, Not More Laws................... 75
CHAPTER 14   Advocate for the Health of It................ 80
CHAPTER 15   It Takes a Sense of Humor.................... 84
About the Author... 89

Acknowledgements

This book would never have seen the light of day without the urging of University of Illinois professor Jocelyn Armstrong. I had been thinking about writing such a book for over 15 years, but never was motivated enough to do it. Professor Armstrong got the ball rolling by listening to me record my thoughts on tape for almost four years. It was with the help of long-time friend, Susan S. Stevens, a former editor for United Press International and for the Chicago City News Bureau, that the words were turned into book form. It is a great honor to have the foreword written by Pulitzer Prize-winning film critic Roger Ebert, whom I've known for over 40 years and first met on the tour of South Africa.

Foreword

by Roger Ebert

I don't know when I first realized that Tom Jones used a wheelchair, but like a lot of people in Champaign-Urbana, I had no idea in the early years. My father and I would be glued to his sportscasts as Tom sat with the other anchors behind the Channel 3 news desk, updating us on Illinois sports. These days it would be a plus for a station to have on-air talent in a wheelchair, but in those days, as Tom notes in his book, management was concerned that viewers would be upset or disturbed or whatever it is that people feel when they are confronted with someone who is not precisely as they expect.

People in wheelchairs were no novelty in Champaign-Urbana, which is where I was born and grew up. In the years after World War Two, many returning servicemen and women with disabilities were looking for a college education, and Prof. Tim Nugent, a legendary educator, founded the University of Illinois Rehabilitation Institute to make it more possible for them. Certainly it helped that the town stood in the middle of flat farmlands, so there were no hills to contend with. My parents and I would often eat at a campus-run cafeteria in one of those Quonset huts that went up during the war, and one of my earlier memories is of its wheelchair ramp, and the students in wheelchairs eating there.

By the late 1950s, while still in high school, I was working part-time as a sports writer for the Champaign-Urbana News-Gazette, and so I would have met Tom and been familiar with his enthusiasm, his talent, and his ability to work as a gifted sportscaster even though he was a high-level paraplegic. Reading his remarkable book, I was struck by a phrase that jumped from the page; he describes himself as "someone who knew how to be disabled." He never for a second allowed his tragic childhood accident to prevent him from obtaining an education, working at a series of demanding jobs, and marrying the wonderful Louise. He was one of the community's best-known and most valuable citizens, and a lot of fun to be around.

Tom describes in his book the 1962 'wheelchair safari' of South Africa and Southern and Northern Rhodesia, as they were then known. As a writer for both the News-Gazette and the Daily Illini campus paper, I was chosen to go along as an assistant, and to file stories and photos to the papers. I also did some play-by-play announcing during the wheelchair sports exhibitions that we put on. Tom could have done that (it was his job, after all!), but he was needed on the team. All of those people became lifelong friends, and I was able to share many memories during a reunion in Champaign-Urbana a few years ago, but Tom and Louise Jones were especially delightful. In 1965, I went back to South Africa on a Rotary Fellowship to the University of Cape Town, and was able to visit Grahamstown and meet again with Tom Knowles, the former RAF pilot who spearheaded the trip. One detail that Jones tactfully doesn't mention is that Knowles had modified his wheelchair so that a case of long-necked beer bottles could fit comfortably under the seat.

Tom is also too kind to mention that I must have been a trial for our group on occasion. I kept getting into political arguments until the tour leader took me aside and informed me firmly that there was a time and a place for everything. I do remember the remarkable hospitality we received there, and I vividly remember, as Tom does, the pilot for the Central African Airways DC-3 who apparently thought he was still in a Spitfire.

Loading our plane became a fixed routine: First the wheelchair athletes would come on board, then the wheelchairs would be lined up down the aisle, then the rest of us would board.

One airport official checked out this arrangement and said it was dangerous. We asked why. "Because in the case of an emergency the people in front won't be able to walk down the aisle." Tom dryly replied, "I don't think that's going to be a problem," and the official eventually came around to the logic of this reply.

Over the years I have caught up with Tom and Louise many times as they rose in their University jobs and became community leaders. They were so kind, as he mentions, to act as hosts for Heather Rose, the young woman who wrote and starred in "Dance Me to My Song" at the first Overlooked Film festival. Her appearance on stage after the screening of that powerful film remains my favorite memory from the festival.

Because of many first-hand contacts and friendships with people with disabilities, and even because I grew up in Champaign-Urbana, a mecca of higher education for those with disabilities, I know something of their lives, challenges, problems and triumphs. Many people do not. There are questions they want to ask, doubts they want to express, things they are too inhibited to ask. By writing about his life so clearly and honesty, Tom has performed a valuable service here. By living his life with such joy, he has performed another.

Roger Ebert

Introduction

How quickly it all can change. One moment I was a robust six-year-old, energetically pedaling a tricycle with two of my many girlfriends riding behind me. The next moment I was down in a street, unable to get up, unable to move my legs.

Two boys, playing with an 'unloaded' rifle, had been 'shooting' at passersby for the past half-hour. One of the teenaged marksmen spotted the towheaded cyclist and his two companions and once again pulled the trigger. This time, the gun was loaded.

I remember it as if it were yesterday.

The bullet entered my sixty-pound body just under the left arm, puncturing a lung, severing my spinal column and emerging about a foot under the right arm. It lodged in the jaw of the girl who was riding behind me, her cheek resting against my shirtless back. It was July and it was hot. My body had slowed the bullet so much that the girl did not even suffer a broken tooth.

The hospital in Carbondale, Ill., my home town, was not equipped to care for a newly injured paraplegic, so I was taken to St. Luke's Hospital in St. Louis, where the attending physician told my folks my chances of survival were one in 10,000.

But I was a tough kid, and that toughness paid off. After months in the hospital, I returned home to a new life, a life altered in the blink of an eye by a boy who didn't know a gun was loaded.

Family support is important when disability occurs, and I was lucky to be surrounded by loving and caring parents and an older brother. My mother was a registered nurse who had a good idea what it would take to allow me to function as a person in a wheelchair in a world made for people who walk. My father, a determined man who had more 'street smarts' than any person I have met, switched to a night shift on the railroad to provide transportation and other help for me.

Support from my brother and friends was vital as I started school, took trumpet lessons, became a rabid sports fan and developed a passion for radio announcing when I was in seventh grade.

With a high degree of independence by the time I entered high school at age fourteen, I was determined to let nothing hold me back. Tommy Jones, as I was called in those days, had the world by the tail.

I played first trumpet in the high school band, edited the newspaper, made the National Honor Society, got my first job as a commercial radio announcer, learned to drive a car, had some very pleasant experiences with girls and was voted by my high school classmates as 'most likely to succeed.'

I earned two degrees from the University of Illinois, enjoyed careers as a television broadcaster and college public affairs specialist, and have been married for more than forty years to a beautiful blonde in a life I am sure never would have been as fulfilling without that July day in 1943—the day "we didn't know the gun was loaded."

What follows are highlights of my life in a wheelchair. I did not write this book to play on emotions. I wrote it with the hope that others who live with disabilities will learn things that will encourage them to become active and productive members of our society where they rightfully belong.

I will try to not preach, although I know I will sometimes. I will try to not lecture, but I have been known to do so on occasion. I will try to show by example that a disability, no matter how severe, is not the end of the world. It is the beginning.

If just one person who reads these words is motivated to overcome a disability, my book is worthwhile.

1

The Gun Wasn't Loaded

The story I am about to tell you, by all rights, should never have been told.

After a bullet from a .22-caliber rifle went in one side of my body and out the other in July of 1943, the doctors told my folks I had a one-in-10,000 chance to live a year.

This is the story of someone who has beaten those odds for over sixty years.

My birth on January 28, 1937, came during what my folks told me was, until 1997, the biggest and most damaging January flood in the history of Southern Illinois. The flood of '37 could be symbolic of the turbulence in my life six years later, when another disaster struck me personally. That is what led me to write this book.

I began kindergarten in 1942 and was looking forward to first grade in the fall of 1943.

In that summer of '43, one of my favorite pastimes was riding a big red tricycle. When I first got the trike, I was not allowed to ride in the streets, so I spent endless hours on the sidewalk, up to the corner and back to our house. I knew every crack in that walk. However, with some begging, which I seemed to be getting better at doing, and many promises that I would be very, very careful, the decision finally was made that allowed me to venture into the street.

We lived in a very quiet, peaceful neighborhood, so there wasn't much automobile traffic to deal with or worry about.

Carbondale summers are hot and dry with lots of sunshine. I'm sure Thursday, July 22, 1943, was that kind of day.

After lunch, I invited two girlfriends who were sisters to take a ride. I had a couple of pennies and we were going to buy candy at Mr. Marvin's store on Springer Street, just a block west of home.

I stood up, pedaling the trike. Ellen sat on the seat just behind me. Her little sister stood on the platform at the rear.

I wanted to show off for the girls, so I said we would take the long way to the store. That meant pedaling south on Almond Street, east on Sycamore, north on Bridge Street and west on Chestnut to Springer. I wanted to show the girls just how strong I was. As the trike-riding trio reached the corner of Bridge and Chestnut, my life changed forever.

A bullet blasted into my shirtless back under the left arm, just missing my heart but puncturing my left lung and severing the spinal cord at the T-5 or 6 level. The bullet emerged from my lower right side and lodged in Ellen's cheek, without breaking a tooth. Without knowing it, I had saved her life.

I remember lying on the brick street, struggling to get up, to continue the trip to Mr. Marvin's store, hearing the girls crying and seeing a crowd gathering. I couldn't understand why my legs didn't work.

I don't remember any pain. I don't remember hearing the crack of the 22-rifle.

Much later, I learned that two teen-age boys from a house 100 yards away had been playing with a gun 'that wasn't loaded' and pretending to shoot everybody who passed by.

I don't remember the trip to Holden Hospital, where I had been born six years earlier. But I remember my mother pacing the hallway, her arms pounding invisible nails, and my aunt Chloe, who also was a nurse, trying to calm her. Nor do I remember the 100-mile ambulance run to a bigger hospital, St. Luke's in St. Louis. Later, they told me the driver made the trip in record time.

In one afternoon, I had changed from a six-year-old tricycle rider to a six-year-old high-level paraplegic.

Shock, pain and fear blur the memory of my hospitalization. I don't remember how long I was there, but my brother said it was a very long time. He had enlisted in the military and been assigned to Jefferson Barracks, which is in St. Louis near the hospital, before shipping overseas with the Army Air Corps. He remembers visiting me in January of 1944, so that meant I was in the hospital for at least six months.

Remember, this was 1943 and very little was known about rehabilitation of a person with such an injury, let alone a six-year-old. Undoubtedly, this played a major part in the long hospital stay.

Dr. Roland Klemme, an orthopedic doctor in St. Louis who did exploratory surgery on me, told the family the odds were one in 10,000 that I would survive for a year. We were told Dr. Klemme was so expert that he had been summoned to England to perform surgery on the king. It has always been exciting to know that the king and I shared a surgeon.

I am always amazed as I think back to the shooting. I remember the noise of St. Louis streetcars, and asking my dad to stop it. He assured me he would.

I have been a St. Louis Cardinal baseball fan for as long as I can remember. But though I was in St. Louis for a good part of the summer, I was unable to attend their games. That would have been a great year to be in the stands. The Cards won 105 games and captured the National League pennant, but they lost the World Series to the Yankees. Games were not televised then and I probably listened to them on the radio, but I don't remember.

I am certain the injury took a major toll on my parents and their marriage. After I returned home, I heard them argue many nights while I was in bed. I don't remember them arguing before I was hurt. One thing I remember was that Dad was angry with Mom, accusing her of allowing me to ride the trike in the street. I felt sad about the arguments, because I knew I was the cause. Their disputes never became violent, and their marriage survived the stress of having a young paraplegic at home and not knowing what was going to happen.

Think of the challenges. They had a child who could not walk, could not control his bladder or bowels, was susceptible to infections and pressure sores, and required to drink eighteen glasses of water a day. However, my folks came from strong stock and were more than ready for the challenges that lay ahead.

Ancestors on my mother's side of the family included John Hart, one of the fifty-six men who signed the Declaration of Independence, and John Hart Crenshaw, who some say kidnapped slaves to work in a salt mine he owned near Equality, Ill. Certainly nothing to be proud of, if indeed it is true.

The Jones family came to America from Ireland in 1797. Franklin Jones took up residence in a small North Carolina community. His descendants gradually moved north, most becoming tobacco farmers in Tennessee. They moved to Illinois when the Civil War started. My immediate family consisted of my railroad worker father, Carl Sr., my nurse mother, Mary Lois, and half-brother, Carl Jr., son of Dad's first wife who had died.

One of my earliest memories at home involved a pig. My name was entered in a raffle, and I won a baby pig. The animal was housed in the basement until it could be taken to Grandpa's farm. It was as friendly as any dog I've ever owned and it loved to have its ears scratched. However, the time came to send my friend to the farm, where soon we were served pork chops.

I remember the world being turned upside down Dec. 7, 1941, when friends and relatives grieved over the Japanese bombing of Pearl Harbor. Carl Junior went into the Army two years later, though I don't remember the war having many adverse effects on the family.

I also don't remember President Franklin Delano Roosevelt being in a wheelchair. I assume some people knew the president had a disability, but it certainly wasn't publicized. I believe President Roosevelt did a great job in office at a very difficult time in our history, but I also believe he would never have been elected if the voting public knew he had a disability severe enough to put him a wheelchair. Given the personal experiences I had in the years following my injury, I don't think he would have had a chance in hell of being elected if it had been widely known that he used a wheelchair much of the time.

The passing years have changed many attitudes. George Wallace was reelected governor of Alabama after being shot and having to use a wheelchair. In the past twenty-five years, we have seen the election at state and national levels of several senators and representatives with disabilities.

Before that bullet went through me I was a typical little boy. I once gave Mom some beautiful tulips. She asked where they came from. I told her they were lying near the sidewalk, even though I had actually picked them from a garden up the block. Mom knew. I was ordered to return the tulips and apologize. I got into more trouble when I traded a small plastic toy to another boy for a great-looking and great-sounding cap pistol. I knew I got the best of the deal. Mom knew differently. I was ordered to return the cap pistol immediately. That was just about the last trouble I got into as a typical, six-year-old boy. The bullet through the spine meant nothing else would be typical for a long, long time.

2

There is a Solution to Every Problem

In 1943, it was impossible for my parents to find a comfortable wheelchair that could be propelled by a six-year-old. My first chair was similar to the one President Franklin Roosevelt used, a large wicker-backed thing with big wheels on the front. It was much, much too big, and difficult for me to push. It didn't fold up and was hard to stuff into a car.

Dad built a steep ramp from the back patio of our house into the kitchen. Going down the ramp was a thrill. Dad attached a handhold so I could ease myself down, but as I grew older I ran the chair at breakneck speed, and that back door took a beating. A ramp also led to the basement and my playroom, but it took two people to get my wheelchair and me up and down the steep steps.

The moment I was shot off that tricycle, I must have become a very old man, at least psychologically. I became more disciplined, more structured, more focused, than any six-year-old should have been.

My parents made me aware of what I had to do to live a successful life. The first grade was on the horizon, but there I was, ready to start school and already behind those who were in my class. Could my parents find a teacher to come to the house? What about braces and crutches that would allow me to try to walk? The steel braces weighed almost as much as I did and covered my body from toes to chest. They were very expensive. Where would my parents find someone to give me proper therapy, without which my legs would stiffen and my muscles would atrophy. They must have been asking: "What if they find a way to cure this paraplegia? If they do, the legs have to be ready to support his body."

Many friends and neighbors visited daily to exercise my legs. They spent hours moving my legs while I sprawled across the dining room table. It was boring, but I tried not to complain because my parents said it was necessary. My dad constantly encouraged me to do more. Wearing the braces, I could lift a foot an inch or two off the floor, but he kept saying, "Walk a little farther." I always replied, "I'm doing the best I can," knowing how much he wanted me to walk. I really wanted to please him and knew how disappointed he was that I was making very little progress.

I did not regain feeling below my waist, and after two years the doctor said there was not much need to keep my legs limber. So, we gave that up. We also gave up the braces because the doctors told my parents that my effort at trying to walk was hard on my heart.

I remember lots of accidents with urine. Later I developed what was called an automatic bladder and knew when it was time to go. I had to drink eighteen glasses of water each day to prevent infections, and it ran right through me. I knew that when nature called, I had to find a bathroom in less than two minutes. Later I learned that spinal cord injured veterans of World War II were given large amounts of water to drink to try and prevent life-threatening bladder and kidney infections. When some of the veterans refused to drink the water, frustrated doctors gave them beer instead. Apparently that beer was a major factor in creating many alcoholics. In my early years, I had no choice. It was lots and lots of water.

Despite the water, bladder infections with fever were frequent. Mom would interrupt her sleep to wake me during the night to force-feed more water. The girls who were riding with me during the shooting visited when I returned home from the hospital. As I hosted the girls, a puddle developed and the girls made a snide remark that caused me to hit them on the knees with a toy guitar. I don't think they ever came back. I recall many adult visitors when I returned home, but not many youngsters. It was also embarrassing for me to go out, because I might pee in my pants, or do something worse.

My dad sent Dr. Klemme a bushel of apples every year. I don't know whether the doctor ever sent us a bill, and there's no way to check on it, but that would have been only one of many extraordinary expenses. Close friends of the family, Dot and Ed Borger, set up a fund to pay bills. Years later, their daughter Sue and I dated steadily. I don't know how much money was contributed to the fund, but I do know the money went toward medication, doctor's visits, wheelchairs, braces, crutches and all else that was required.

My father was an engine lister for the Illinois Central Railroad, an office job he never seemed to enjoy, although he worked for the IC for almost forty years. My mother was a registered nurse and worked in a doctor's office. Even if they were not able to pay all the bills themselves, they made up for it in other ways. I had parents who were determined that I would not end up sitting in the house, then move to a nursing home when they died. Motivation they gave me made me able to do what I did all these years. They always said the easy way out was not the answer to what I would face.

When I first came home from the hospital, my mother stopped working at the doctor's office to assume most of the responsibility for my care. Also, a young lady named Marjorie Kelly served as a kind of babysitter or a relief caregiver.

Dad had wanted to follow in Grandpa's footsteps and become a mainline engineer, which paid as much as $1,200 a month during the Depression. But that would have required transfer to another town. Perhaps my injury put a stop to those plans. It was never talked about. Shortly after I was injured, he took the night shift. I believe it was to ease the burden on my mother, but they never said. He never seemed to get enough sleep, especially when I was in junior high school. After I was able to attend a regular school, he would arrive home from work, eat a bowl of cereal, load me into the car and take me there. When I started high school, he often returned between each class to make sure I got from one to another. It took a year or two for him to trust my classmates to pull me up the stairs for classes on the second floor.

In my early years rather attractive young teachers home-schooled me when I was well enough. By third grade my report card indicates I was never absent or tardy. Aside from a period at a special school in Chicago I was home-schooled until I was ready for seventh grade. Brush School in Carbondale was inaccessible to a person in a wheelchair. I went to a real school building in Carbondale for junior high, or seventh and eighth grade. At that time I was the only person in Carbondale who attended school in a wheelchair. The junior high had a ground-level entrance and was on one floor. My dad or mom would drive me to school, and I would go through a regular class day. After school, I would get a ride home.

I had played trumpet for a couple of years—my dad wanted me to be another Harry James, and figured it was good for my lungs. Since the bullet had punctured one lung, there had been a concern about its functioning. The trumpet allowed me to become a schoolboy star. I was big at pageants. I'm not sure how good I was, but I was a boy in a wheelchair playing the trumpet, and that apparently was appealing.

One of my favorite activities in junior high was physical education. Most of the time I had the gym to myself and would zip up and down the floor to shoot baskets. Since I was the only player on the court, my team always won. Gym class became especially fun when the teacher, also the basketball coach, had all the able-bodied players sit on little carts with wheels that they pushed with their feet. We played five-on-five basketball. Since I was in my chair, I was the seven-footer in this league. Everyone wanted me on his team! I was the star!

I remember with great fondness Jimmy Waldrop, who was in all of my junior high classes. Jimmy was assigned to help me when I had to leave class and get to the bathroom. I carried a metal urinal in a bag on the back of my wheelchair. It was called a 'duck' because of the long neck that protruded from the rounded bottom. The procedure was fraught with danger, because if I felt the urge to go when classes were changing or the hallway or bathroom was crowded, I might not make it in time. This happened on occasion, leaving me with wet pants and great embarrassment. I continued using that system through most of high school. By high school I was skilled enough and fast enough to work the plan on my own. During my high school years, I also started using an external collection device, which worked well except for occasions when the urine backed up in the device, and there I would be, again in wet pants and embarrassed.

My pants were wet when a picture was taken my senior year. In a class of ninety I was fortunate enough to be voted the boy most likely to succeed. I was very proud. And yet, I thought, "Just how am I going to succeed at anything if I always have wet pants?"

Those porcelain 'ducks' served me well at night. At bedtime, I would put one in place beside me in bed. I had to stay in that position all night—but it worked! I used that system until 1980, when something better came along.

My philosophy has always been, "There is a solution to every problem." If you don't give up and keep working at it, you will eventually find a way. How many times in your life have you been forced to do something you really didn't want to do, but you knew it had to be done? One of my philosophies: I can stand to do anything for a short period of time, if I know it will lead to something better.

By the way, that porcelain duck allowed me to become a twelve-year-old paid counselor at a camp for crippled children at Giant City State Park. I stayed several nights and did not wet the bed.

Dan Kimmel, a student who helped me up and down stairs in high school was on the basketball team. He later became a lawyer, then a judge. We met again a few years ago, and he told me that his years of helping me allowed him to assist an elderly family member when she needed a wheelchair. You never know how you affect others in your life.

I never enjoyed school. I hated to get up early and hated the regimen. But there were parts I did enjoy. Meeting other students, playing in the band, working on the newspaper, competing in speech contests—all of those things were terrific. I've been almost amazed that someone who disliked school so much could receive two degrees from the University of Illinois and teach at the same university for seven years. However, I knew how important an education was for me.

Had I not been injured, I would never have advanced past high school. I most likely would have worked on the railroad. I would have played softball. I would have enjoyed beer with the guys every Saturday night. More importantly, I would never have met and married Louise, a cherished mate and companion for more than forty years.

> *Marjorie Kelly Martin, babysitter and family friend:*
> *"I remember him as a typical little boy and I loved him like a little brother...*
> *I was heartbroken, as were his family and friends, when the accident happened. I spent the evening with the family, at the hospital in Carbondale, before he was taken to a hospital in St. Louis."*

3

A Cardinal Fan in Cub Territory

Home schooling lasted for perhaps two years, with pretty teachers who kept my attention and apparently gave me a good educational foundation. Then this Cardinal fan moved to Cub territory in Chicago. My parents sent me to the Illinois Children's Hospital School, blocks from Wrigley Field. My folks must have felt that rehabilitation would come faster and better at a hospital school with nurses, social workers and doctors perhaps better prepared to work with a person in my condition.

I made friends quickly and easily. We played baseball on the roof of the seven-story building, and I often wondered what persons walking along the street below thought when one of our home runs came bouncing down from above. I won a water-drinking contest, but embarrassment replaced jubilation when a puddle formed beneath my wheelchair. Why in the world do I remember stuff like this?

Sometimes my folks would visit for a weekend and take me to a Cubs game. Even though it was just to see the Cubs, what a thrill it was for me to push my chair from the hospital school at 2551 N. Clark Street to Wrigley Field.

To control my bladder a doctor at the school gave me a clamp that attached to the penis and shut off urination. The clamp made my penis swell if I left it in place too long. At the same time the urine would back up into my bladder and set up a good environment for infection. I have not used that clamp since I left the hospital school. Rehabilitation techniques were not too great in the 1940s.

While I was at the school my legs began to spasm so severely that I even had trouble sleeping. We were told an operation available at the Illinois Research Hospital would cut the nerves and relieve the spasms. My parents, with my approval, decided to go ahead with the surgery, even though the cut nerves would prevent my ever walking, even if a cure was found for paraplegia. The surgery was performed, and I have not had spasms since. Since a cure for paraplegia has not been found, the decision to cut the nerves was the right one.

My stay at the school was for no more than 18 months. Development of a pressure area concluded it. To treat the spot a heat lamp was placed over the area while I slept. One night I turned and placed one of my legs directly on the heating element, but having no feeling below the waist, I did not know I was being burned until I awoke and smelled meat cooking. The meat was on my leg and foot. Next morning I watched as a doctor removed damaged tissue down to the bone. Healing took a long time, and my parents removed me from the school shortly after the burning. Despite the injury, the residential school gave me a tremendous opportunity to associate with other young people my age. Home schooling resumed after I returned to Carbondale, and my circle of friends grew. Because of my passion for baseball, Dad mapped out a ball diamond in a field near our house. Kids came out of the woodwork, and they all wanted to play. All the other players were able-bodied, and I was the only one who used a wheelchair. I was a very good hitter, but because of my bad balance I batted with one hand, using a regular-size bat. When I hit the ball I had someone run the bases for me. In the field I usually played first base, and opposing batters were not allowed to bunt. What a great time that was!

One day another boy, Richard Kelly, made an errant throw that knocked out one of my permanent front teeth. Today a dentist probably would put that tooth back in place. Then, apparently, the only choice was to put in a partial.

Dad bought me a real St. Louis Cardinal baseball uniform that I still have. Dad knew it would please me if I could meet some of my baseball heroes, so he made arrangements for me to sit at the entrance to the Cardinal dressing room at old Sportsman's Park in St. Louis and meet the players as they headed to the field. Stan Musial, Enos Slaughter, Del Rice, Whitey Kurowsky and Nippy Jones were among the players who shook my hand and chatted. In fact, my baseball uniform carries Nippy's old number, three.

During one of our trips to St. Louis, I saw Harry Caray and his son, Skip. The Cardinal announcer who made games come alive on radio was in his Buick convertible when we pulled up next to it at a stop sign near the ballpark. Years later, Caray and I sat across a table from each other at a Big Ten basketball luncheon in Chicago, but we were not close enough to speak. Dad had written to Caray, asking if I could visit him in the radio booth. The answer was a polite no, but Caray wrote and wished me well. I still have that letter. When I heard him in 1945, I wanted to be a major league baseball announcer. Sadly, I was never able to achieve that goal, and never got to shake the hand of the man I admired so much. In fact, that admiration carried over when Caray finished his career broadcasting for the Cubs. I actually listened to some really bad Cub teams because he made the game so exciting.

> *Dr. Dale Jones, friend since their childhood:*
> *"I never remember Tom being down. His disability was never a handicap. He was very intense, compulsive, focused and goal-oriented. He was, as a young boy growing up, independent and developed an intense independent spirit. He has maintained this independence throughout his adult life. He has been able to do things and accomplish things that most people in his situation would not have been able to do."*

4

A Career in Radio Beckons

I became hooked on broadcasting when I was eleven or twelve, and my brother took me to radio station WAVA in Ava, Ill., where he worked weekends as an announcer. He let me read the weather forecast! It was my first real experience in broadcasting, and I loved it. My brother has a great voice and was a terrific announcer, but his interests were in other areas. He became a teacher, then principal, then assistant superintendent of Carbondale grade schools.

About the time I started junior high there were family discussions about what I could do when I graduated from high school.

Having listened to Cardinal baseball games religiously, I thought it would be great to be a baseball announcer or radio announcer. This was before much television. But I also thought it would be glamorous to be a taxicab driver. I have no idea why. So I mulled over the two ideas until one day somebody told me that taxi drivers sometimes had to leave the car and carry groceries into a house or help people in or out of the cab. I realized I would be unable to do that, so the only thing left was announcing. As a result, I made a career decision before I entered my teenage years. I was going to be a radio announcer and hoped some day to replace Harry Caray. My family said it was a good choice and encouraged me. My father, mother and brother all basically said, "If that's what you want to do, let's try it."

Before graduating from eighth grade I began to rehearse in the back bedroom of our home, where I had a small basketball hoop above the door. I used a small rubber ball, and played basketball games and announced them at the same time. I also kept score for Cardinal baseball games while listening to them on the radio. Long after the season was over, I recreated games from my official scorebook while pretending to broadcast on the radio.

When we installed our first television set—I think it was a Zenith with a twelve-inch screen—I realized there was something other than radio announcing. Of course I had no idea that my future career would be in television. I began public address announcing for the high school basketball and football teams. Doing PA work for basketball wasn't too difficult because I could get out of my wheelchair and climb up in the bleachers where the microphone was located.

Football was more complicated. The press box at the field was about twenty feet in the air, with a ladder that went straight up from the ground. Dad, ingenious person that he was, nailed a two-by-four to the top of the press box, attached a pulley to the board and a rope around the pulley. The rope was long enough to reach the ground and securely tie around my wheelchair. Two strong young men hoisted me that twenty feet to the press box. Someone would reach out and pull in my wheelchair. It's not bad going up, but think about going down!

Baseball was my number one announcing goal, but no high school baseball games were broadcast on radio at that time. That didn't stop me from honing my skill. Dad built a platform behind the backstop at the high school field to position me higher than home plate and permit me to see the entire field. I took my tape recorder, and announced games. Though those games were never broadcast, I listened to the tapes and tried to improve. It was good practice.

I entered speech contests because a high school speech teacher said it would be good experience for someone who wanted to be a radio announcer. She must have seen something in my ability because I won the state radio speaking contest as a freshman. WILL, the University of Illinois station, recorded that speech and sent me a record. I could not believe how I sounded. The twang. The accent. I was nasal. What a disappointment. "I can't be a radio announcer and sound like this." I went to work using a tape recorder and practiced to rid myself of that terrible sound.

Next year, despite my much-improved voice, I finished fifth at the state meet. Because of work commitments I never again competed in state speech contests. A few years later Roger Ebert, a young man from Urbana, won the same state speech contest.

I joined the staff of the high school newspaper as a general assignment reporter when I was a freshman. During my sophomore year I was the paper's sports reporter, and during my junior year I was assistant editor. That meant I was editor of The Monitor during my senior year. One editorial I wrote was titled, "Don't Kiss in the Halls." My, how times have changed!

Winning first place in the speech contest made me even more set on becoming an announcer. And it made me eager to start. My father drove me to many stations in and around Carbondale as I tried for a job. Put yourself in a station manager's position. You see somebody in a wheelchair who is too young to drive, who has no commercial radio experience but is asking for a job. About the only thing I could hang my hat on was that contest-winning radio speech.

We finally arrived at WFRX in West Frankfort, thirty-five or forty miles from Carbondale. Bob Veach, the station manager, said he'd take a chance on me and gave me a weekend announcing job. I read news and sports and played records. Most of the music came from seventy-eight rpm records, which are not even produced today. I also took requests for songs from people who drove up to the station. That may have been the very first drive-in music request show. Mom and Dad took turns driving me to the station on Saturdays and Sundays. I also did high school news on WCIL in Carbondale for about five minutes every Saturday morning. The host of that show was a high school upperclassman named John Coleman, whose path I would cross again in a few years. This is the same John Coleman who gained national fame as a weatherman on ABC Television's Good Morning America, the same John Coleman who started cable television's The Weather Channel.

First at WFRX, then WCIL, I put high school basketball games on tape. There were no FM stations then and both AM stations signed off at sunset, so the games would have to wait to be broadcast until the next day.

Trumpet lessons continued, and I played in the band through high school. I participated in trumpet competitions, never winning the top prize but enjoying it. Several of us formed a little dance band that played for the Elks, Moose and other club events.

Somehow I found time enough to study, and was elected to the National Honor Society. I graduated seventh in my class of ninety.

Surgery had stopped the spasms in my legs, but curvature of the spine followed. My muscles were not developed because I was injured at such an early age, and the curvature developed as my body matured. For a year or two I wore a corset-like device to try and hold me straight. The corset worked for awhile, but back pain and my balance worsened as I grew. A doctor recommended an orthopedic brace company in St. Louis. The B & H Brace Shop made me a steel and leather back brace that fit around my hips and rose to just under my armpits. A fabric front closed it. The brace straightened me in good fashion. We had to replace it every two or three years at a cost of several hundred dollars and it was not covered by insurance.

A brace like that on someone who has no feeling below the waist can create dangerous pressure sores. Until one's skin toughens, one has a good chance of developing serious skin problems. So my dear mother, good nurse that she was, taught me to be a regular watchdog of my skin. That type of brace had worked for a long time with few problems, and by 1983 I had worn out five or six. The brace-makers changed the configuration each time because the curvature became worse. I'll discuss later how and why I got rid of the braces.

Shortly after my sixteenth birthday we bought hand controls for the family car. They were primitive compared to today's devices, but they worked. The control was structured like a motorcycle grip. A wire ran through a housing and attached to the accelerator behind the firewall under the steering wheel. It was a big problem in winter when cold weather stiffened oil in the housing. Sometimes it was impossible to move the grip and feed the gas. Again, Dad found a solution. He gave me a walking cane to carry in the car. If I was unable to push the accelerator, I could at least get home by pushing on the gas pedal with the walking cane. Fortunately, today's hand controls don't require a cane to function.

When I took my driver's test the examiner gave me directions—turn right, or whatever. Then, he said, "I'm going to yell, 'Stop!' I want to see how fast you can do it." I said, "OK." He did, and I did. He hit his head on the windshield, sat back, turned to me and said, "You pass." I didn't even have to parallel park.

I took my first date to a drive-in movie, but my dad was in the back seat to make certain I could drive at night. I probably put my arm around my girlfriend, Sue Borger, but my dad's presence prevented anything further. Being a fairly shy person, I am sure nothing else would have happened anyway.

A double date for my senior prom came to an inauspicious end. I was co-host and announcer at a theater premier after the dance. Sue and I double-dated with another couple, and I drove. After the big events, I dropped off the other couple, took Sue home and pulled into my own driveway. I turned around to get my chair out of the back seat. It was not there. It was in the trunk. In my spiffy gray suit, I scooted onto the oil-covered rock driveway to the car trunk. Somehow I managed to lift the more than fifty-pound wheelchair out of the trunk and got inside before Dad got home from work shortly after seven a.m. I never told my parents.

It was time to give serious consideration to what to do after high school. In those days, Southern Illinois University in Carbondale was not a wheelchair-accessible campus, though today the school has one of the top programs in the country for persons with disabilities.

The owner of WCIL offered me the chief announcer's job for the princely sum of a dollar an hour for a forty-eight-hour week. That wasn't bad money for an eighteen-year-old in 1955, and I would have been able to live at home. I would have been a big fish in a small pond. Yet, I knew I needed a college education.

We found out about a program at the University of Illinois in Champaign that Tim Nugent had developed a few years earlier. I started writing him, then I began calling him. Tim said he could admit a limited number of students with disabilities because he had a quota! So, I continued to pester him with letters and calls. Finally—I don't think it was much more than a month before the start of classes—Tim said, "You can come." I am certain he allowed me to enroll just to stop the letters and calls. Sometimes it pays to be a pest.

Many high school classmates became life-long friends. Dale Jones, no relation, became a doctor in Decatur. Marris Lingle pitched for SIU and had a long career with the railroad. We played basketball and baseball together in the yard. I met many good people through announcing, too. One was Abe Martin, who had coached basketball, football and baseball at SIUC. Another was John Coleman, who was two years ahead of me in high school and was an announcer on Carbondale station WCIL. As he left the PA jobs in high school, I took over. We linked up again in Champaign at WCIA television in 1957. I met Herrin High School basketball coach Ledio Cabutti while audio taping games. He became Champaign High coach my second year at the U of I, and our friendship has continued through the years.

The PA announcer job got me into trouble once. It was my senior year and we were playing Murphysboro in the season-ending football game. Even though Murphysboro was a smaller town, the Red Devils beat the Terriers on a regular basis. Because so many people wanted to see the game, it was played at SIU's football stadium. The game was coming down to the last seconds, with Carbondale leading 7-0. Carbondale had the ball but was going in the opposite direction of the scoreboard and clock. As a result, Terrier players did not know how much time was left in the game. So I started to count down 30 seconds, 29 seconds, 28 seconds. Everyone in the stadium could hear me. This didn't set very well with the Murphysboro fans, but Carbondale won the game, 7 to 0.

Next week the Murphysboro principal wrote a nasty letter to the Carbondale principal, talking about the 'poor sportsmanship' showed by the announcer. My principal called me in and said, "I should be reprimanding you, but since we beat Murphysboro so seldom, I'll just tell you that's probably not a good thing you did and you shouldn't do it again." Then we laughed because, being a senior, I would not have a chance to do it again anyway.

High school girlfriend Sue Borger Sutton:
"All the years I've known Tom I've never heard him mention the word limitation. He still presents that infectious smile and wonderful sense of humor. Tom's strength, determination and positive attitude helped me in coping with the loss of my son at age 17 and with my own chronic illness. My relationship with Tom has been a great influence on my life!"

Coach Lee Cabutti:
"Tom is an outstanding example that one can succeed in spite of having some limitations...He is the type of person that is always doing something for others, and it is difficult to do favors for him. Nominating him and seeing him inducted into the Illinois Basketball Coaches Hall of Fame in the area of sports media was a great thrill for me."

5

First College, Then Television

The decision to move about 200 miles to the north was agonizing. I was a small town boy. Population signs at the edge of Carbondale said 10,300. I was leaving my home, my parents, brother and many good friends. I also had to leave my girlfriend, Sue Borger, who went to nursing school in St. Louis. But it was time to move on.

One of my first activities in Champaign was what Tim Nugent called "functional training week." It was required of all students with disabilities before class registration. It was a time to learn about campus, get advice on classes, meet new friends, play games, and most of all, prove to Tim and his staff that you could function on your own.

"You don't let anybody push your wheelchair," Nugent told us, "You push yourself."

Most of us didn't like functional training week, but it made us better able to survive and succeed in these new surroundings. Functional training week no longer exists, and today's students are worse off due to its demise.

Most of the students with disabilities at the U of I in the fifties either had spinal cord injuries or polio. There were exceptions. Tom Lindy had some kind of spastic disability. He needed help at mealtime, but he used a standard wheelchair that he pushed backwards with one foot. Despite his severe disability, Tom earned a doctorate. He typed every word of his own thesis, holding in his teeth a pencil that he laboriously placed, letter by letter, in a grid fashioned over a typewriter keyboard. I know this firsthand because he typed the whole thesis late into many nights, sitting in front of my dorm room.

Today those coming to campus with disabilities have experienced a broader range of conditions, many much more limiting and requiring many forms of assistance in order for the student to succeed.

During my first two years of college I lived in tarpaper shacks brought from military bases originally to house the overflow of World War II veterans. They were drafty and cold in the winter, hot in the summer. They had ramps on each end and a community bathroom in the middle. We were told that if a building caught fire, it would burn down in four minutes. I really don't think today's students would put up with that kind of sub-standard living arrangement. We were just happy to be able to go to college, under any circumstances.

The staff tried to pair able-bodied students with roommates who had disabilities. I had great luck. Two of my three roommates during my entire college career are still good friends.

Dick Herbst, a ceramics engineer, was my first roommate. Dick and wife Donna, who had five lovely daughters, are now in retirement, but we still see each other from time to time. John Kurinsky and wife Judy now live in Florida in retirement, and we delight in breaking bread together when they travel to their former home in Wisconsin, where John managed a steel company plant.

I soon became aware that the learning environment in college was much different than in high school. Nugent had me sign up for a physiology class, telling me it would teach me about my body. The amount I learned was reflected in the grade, one of two Ds I received in four years of college.

That D put me on academic probation for my second semester. Many of the class experiments were tough to perform in a wheelchair. In one, students had to run up and down steps and then be measured to learn what effect this had on their bodies. I think I had to push my chair up and down the hall as some sort of substitute.

A question on the final exam was, "You're walking down the street, and you stub your toe. Explain what happens." Since I hadn't walked or stubbed my toe since I was six, I answered that it hurts. Was that wrong?

Some of my bad grades were caused by the fact I was trying to do too much. Wheelchair football was one of the most enjoyable parts of my freshman year, but it took a lot of time. We practiced during the week and played each Saturday morning in the University Armory. Though I had poor balance and fell out of my chair often, I was fast. During the very first play of the very first game, Dean Nosker threw me a long pass and I completed what turned out to be a sixty-yard touchdown. I think it was probably the only touchdown I scored all year.

During that first semester I became a regular disc jockey at WPGU, the campus student station. Also, I did the play-by-play announcing for Illini baseball games on WPGU, and had a job checking food passes in the dormitory to help with meal costs.

After the wheelchair football season, I started playing basketball with the famous Gizz Kids team. I made the starting line-up as a guard and went on several long road trips.

I remember trips to Chicago, Cleveland, St. Louis and Kansas City. On that Kansas City trip our bus broke down on a Sunday morning, just a few minutes after we left campus. Then an engine failed near Grinnell, Iowa, where we stayed in a very old hotel for an extra day until the bus could be fixed. Needless to say, this hotel was not at all accessible for a bunch of people in wheelchairs, but we managed. What fun those trips were.

Plus, I had a date or two. I wasn't very successful at romance my freshman year. One woman became a nun several years after she dated me.

Dad told me I had to quit playing basketball until I was removed from probation. I had no choice. Father knows best. I'd also begun having more bladder infections. Stress was part of the problem and I probably wasn't drinking my 18 glasses of water a day.

I was taken off probation the second semester and that spring I got a call from John Coleman at WCIA-TV, asking if I would do a voice-over commercial for a politician. I was paid a small amount for my first association with Channel 3. I also played trumpet at several events, including a big picnic for all students with disabilities. Shortly after that experience, the horn went into the case where it remains to this day. Sorry Dad, I didn't have the talent or the desire to become the next Harry James.

During the summer prior to university year number two, I returned home and worked almost full-time at WCIL, where my brother and I were pretty much the entire announcing staff. On one of the DJ shows, I took telephone requests and a few dates resulted. The girls didn't know I was in a wheelchair until I picked them up. It was a little discouraging when very few second dates materialized. Sue was still in nursing school, and it was obvious that our relationship had no future. We agreed it would be best if we dated others.

In the fall I returned to the U of I and wheelchair football but played no more basketball. I still worked the food checker job along with the air shift at WPGU. I made decent grades and waited anxiously for the wheelchair baseball season to begin in the spring.

Then John Coleman called again. He said WCIA had a booth announcing job open and wanted me to audition. Since I didn't have a car, John gave me a ride to the station for the audition. I got the job in March of 1957. But how was I going to get to work? The station was three miles from the dormitory, and there was no accessible bus service in Champaign at the time. Dad and Mom sold me their car, accepting small payments each month from the money I made at WCIA.

For the rest of the semester I worked five or six days a week, from four until sign-off, which was around midnight. Getting up for an eight or nine o'clock class was somewhat difficult. But hey, I was twenty years old, I was full of excitement and they were paying me $1 an hour. I bought new clothes. They widened a stall in the bathroom at the station so my wheelchair would fit. And they gave me a $.25 raise after my three-month trial period.

That wider bathroom stall was the only accommodation made at the station to allow me to work there. The building housing the station was a former candy warehouse and on one level. There were no steps to enter, and it was totally flat inside. My workstation in the newsroom consisted of a desk and a manual typewriter on a pullout panel. The wire room was small, but big enough for me to take news from the United Press International printer.

I worked almost every day all summer in 1957. At some point management put me on camera to read copy for the 'News Final,' which I presented after the late movie. I did that for several months before management said I would be doing some weekend sports programs. Sports Director Tom Schoendienst needed weekend relief, so I was assigned to do the Sunday night sports.

When I was hired, station officials told me they did not want to show the wheelchair on camera. I wasn't going to upset the apple cart, but asked why. Station Manager James Fielding said he did not want the audience to feel WCIA was trying to gain its sympathy by showing a staff member who used a wheelchair. That was a totally inappropriate response. But it was 1957, and people with disabilities had not been out in public doing things on a regular basis. So, every time I appeared on TV I would transfer out of my wheelchair into a regular straight-backed chair and sit behind a desk. It took several years, but this attitude would change later because of the kinds of programs I did during my nineteen and a half years at the station.

Tim Nugent, director emeritus of the Rehabilitation Education Center at the University of Illinois:

"That he survived and became so active and successful throughout these many years is somewhat of a miracle. Much of the knowledge and equipment and many of the services available today did not exist at the time of his injury. This is a real tribute to his parents and others who worked with him."

Richard Herbst, Tom's first roommate:

"I'm sure a large measure of our success as roommates was Tom's upbeat spirit, wiry sense of humor and constancy. I don't ever remember exchanging a cross word or having a mean thought."

John Kurinsky, Tom's second roommate:

"While we were in school I always marveled at Tom's unique ability to spend little time studying and get high grades on his tests and finals. Here's a man who worked almost forty hours a week, went to school, was involved in numerous school activities, spent time with his girlfriend (now wife) and still did very well academically. One characteristic about Tom is that he is a very independent person. There is little he asks or wants anyone to do for him. He is always willing to give more than he expects to receive; perhaps this is what has helped make him a very successful person throughout his life."

6

The Love of My Life

A special young woman who used a wheelchair came to the U of I in the new freshman class in the fall of 1957. I first saw her pretty face when a Rehabilitation Services bus passed me while I sat at the corner waiting for the light to change at Fourth Street and Gregory Drive, across the street from Huff Gym. She looked out the window at me and smiled. I was excited. Though I'd had a few dates at college before that, nothing extraordinary had occurred in my love life.

A while later I took a group of new students, including that young woman, around campus to show everyone the various classrooms and the accessible entrances. A few days later I was sitting in Tim Nugent's office when I saw this beautiful young lady pass by. I asked Tim for her name. He told me Louise Fortman was one of the new students on campus. Tim says that I told him, "I'm going to marry that woman some day." I don't remember saying that, but Tim never hesitates to tell the story. I have been known to make quick decisions.

A few days later Louise agreed to be my date at the annual Welcome New Student Picnic at Lake Springfield. A relationship began that September Sunday in 1957 that has lasted 44 years.

Louise had suffered from polio a year or two before Jonas Salk discovered the vaccine. Her sister got it first, but recovered fully and quickly. Louise spent six weeks in an iron lung and never regained the use of her legs, except for one foot. After high school Louise had been working full-time with the 3M Company for about three months and trying to figure out what to do with the rest of her life. Polio helped her decide to go to college. She graduated from the U of I with a history degree.

Since I had purchased my folks' car when I landed the job at Channel 3, Louise and I could go to drive-in movies and other places instead of simply holding hands in the dormitory. The two-door green Chevrolet's back seat could accommodate two wheelchairs. As the years rolled by, finding cars with that much room in the back became very difficult.

Working almost full time while going to school limited my dating to Saturdays and Sundays. A short time later, I started doing weekend sports, and that cramped my dating even further, but not my growing affection for Louise. Despite the time limitations we became serious as the summer of 1958 approached. Louise went home to Hinsdale, where she lived with her mother. I stayed in Champaign and worked at the TV station but was lonely because our relationship had developed into something more than friendship.

My external collection device weighed on my mind. How would she react if urine leaked from the device or if I was gassy? I learned the answer that summer, after she invited me to visit her and her family. While we were out one evening, my external collection device filled and needed to be emptied. I stopped the car in a private place and asked Louise, "I'm going to have to do this, do you mind?" Her answer was, "No, not at all." That cleared a big hurdle. What a relief! Louise has been caring and loving in such situations ever since.

That was my first extended time with Louise's mother, Emmy. She had come to this country from Germany in the 1920s and married John Fortman, who also emigrated from Germany. I also met Louise's younger sister, Mary, a teenager, and her older brother, Jack, who held two engineering degrees from the U of I. John Fortman, who was a trumpet player, was band director at Father Flanagan's Boys Town in Omaha shortly after coming to this country. Louise was thirteen when her father died.

That fall, a year after I met Louise, I asked her for the first time to marry me. I was starting my senior year and she was starting her sophomore year. It seemed like a good thing to do. At first she said, "No, not yet." But I held out hope and asked several times during that fall and winter. My ego was a little bruised from never hearing "yes." She finally said that word one night when we were parked in what used to be the parking lot of the old Cole Hospital, at Church and Prospect in Champaign. I'm sure most of us remember where we were when our future wife said yes. I had decided it would be the last time I'd ask, but that is probably not the case.

But before marrying we had to figure out how to make our marriage work. Today, we hear many stories about people with disabilities marrying—even those who need attendant care. However, in 1959 it was a great concern, at least to me. How would two people in wheelchairs live by themselves, even though I had been totally independent for years? We were going to have to do our own grocery shopping. We would have to do our cleaning and cooking and all the other things that need to be done when keeping house. Where would we live? What about children?

My mother suggested I was rushing into something with Louise, who was only the second woman with whom I'd had a serious relationship. "I think it would be wise for you to wait at least a year, and maybe two, after graduation before you get married," my mother said. She even offered me money to travel and do other things after I finished school.

Traveling was out, because Channel 3 offered me a full-time job after I graduated that spring. I told my mother, "This is a job I really want to do." Since I was going to be in Champaign anyway and since Louise had two years of school left, I said marriage would be good for both of us. Louise talked about not finishing college, but I told her, "If we get married, you've got to finish school. That's just part of the deal." She visited my family in Carbondale, and won them over.

We decided to take another plunge at the same time and build a house. A subdivision called Holiday Park was being planned in West Champaign, and to keep costs down, the developer put up what were called pre-cut homes, with limited choices. We bought a lot and the house for $10,300 and fortunately didn't need a down payment. Our monthly payments, including taxes, interest and principle were less than $90. Our salesman went out of his way to help us make the home as accessible as it could be to persons in wheelchairs. The builders sloped the sidewalk up to the front door's ground-level entrance. A small patio in back made for another ground-level entrance. The bathroom door was made a little wider than normal.

Louise was doing secretarial work part-time in the Division of Rehab Education Services at the U of I, and I made either $1.75 or $2 an hour at the TV station. When we were married, we asked family and friends for gifts for our home. We received a refrigerator and a washer-dryer, which really helped.

Before our wedding on Aug. 15, 1959, we had to give religion deep thought. Louise was raised Catholic and I was not going to convert, so I had to take instruction in Catholic beliefs and principles as a requirement for marriage in her church.

I don't recall whether I had to agree that any children would be raised Catholic, but our physical conditions made us question whether we would or even could have them. Could I produce enough sperm? And, with Louise having been in an iron lung for six weeks, how difficult would it be for her to carry a child for nine months? Now, of course, even high-level paraplegics can father children through various methods and quadriplegic women carry children to full term. I am sure we could have discovered something that would have worked, but at that point in our marriage we were not interested enough to explore the possibilities.

We each had a career and were busy dealing with our own wants. Louise, a more laid-back person than I, wasn't concerned. If children came, fine. If not, also fine. Later on, I decided I would not have been a very good father because I am not very patient in some ways. Louise would have made a terrific mother.

My brother was best man at our wedding. My mom and dad were there, as were Louise's mother, brother, sister and many other relatives. The wedding was in St. Isaac Jogues Catholic Church in Hinsdale, Louise's home church. It was a wonderful, beautiful event. After the reception Louise and I drove straight home, because I had to work the next day. Louise has never said she was bothered that we did not have a honeymoon after the wedding. We did get to honeymoon the following summer, when my two-week vacation allowed us enough time to drive to San Francisco.

Ours was the third home finished in Holiday Park, and the streets were not put in. When we arrived after our wedding it had been raining, and we hoped the car would not get stuck in the mud. We had to drive up to the back door in order to get into the house, but we were able to spend our first night of marriage in our own home.

John Coleman, who lived in the area, volunteered to hang our curtains after we moved in. He and other friends were very important. Chuck and Adrienne Dahncke, who graduated with me in 1959, were married shortly before we were. Dean and Lola Nosker were a year ahead of me in school, and Paul Luedtke and his family were involved in that support system as well as being life-long friends. Luedtke was and has continued to be one of our community's business leaders.

Since Louise and I did not have a lot of money, most of our entertainment was watching television. We decided we needed a pet to expand our lives. I always had a dog while growing up, and Louise's father trained German shepherds. I knew I couldn't go to the Humane Society without coming home with several animals, so we decided to go to a breeder and chose a dachshund. A puppy named Sam became the third member of the Jones household in 1960.

I still have scars on my fingers from the times Sam objected to my method of discipline. When he was about five he developed back problems and required surgery. He lived for seven years after that and continued to be one of the most spirited family members.

In 1960 we bought our first new car, a Chevrolet Impala without air conditioning. That made our delayed honeymoon trip to California somewhat uncomfortable because the six-cylinder engine could not take us across the desert fast enough!

Louise and I decided it would be better for us if we had a third person on such a long trip. I asked a Channel 3 engineer, who was single, if he'd help with the driving and be there in case of some sort of emergency. We paid for all the gasoline, and he paid for his own motel rooms. Most motels were not made to be accessible to persons in wheelchairs in the early 1960s, so he also checked out the rooms to make sure our wheelchairs would fit.

At the time, it was quite adventurous for two persons in wheelchairs to undertake such a trip, and we felt it was a great accomplishment. We've been to San Francisco several times since, and it's most likely my favorite city in this country.

Back in Champaign I joined several other U of I alumni on a basketball team called The Black Knights. We played in Chicago, St. Louis, St. Joseph, Mo., Cleveland, Ohio and smaller communities. We paid our own expenses, and carpooled.

Paul Luedtke was our equipment boy and one of our biggest boosters. The games drew 800 to 1,000 people and we used our small cut of the gate to help pay expenses. I especially remember a game at LeRoy. I was a good shooter and decided to show off. So every time my teammates passed me the ball I took it across the centerline, and about halfway to the free-throw circle I'd fire away with a two-handed push shot. I hit at least four in a row and waited for the applause. The audience sat on its hands. I was about as hot as I've ever been shooting a basketball, but got absolutely no praise. I wondered if they thought I did that on a regular basis. My teammates and I finally decided the audience just didn't understand what was going on. What a three-point shooter I would be in today's game.

Most of our exhibition games were against teams made up of folks who lived in that community and had little or no wheelchair-pushing experience. Normally, we would spot them about fifty points and then work to beat them. The games educated the public about what people who used wheelchairs could do. Our record was as good as the Harlem Globetrotters. I don't recall ever losing one of those games.

The university offered wheelchair baseball, football and basketball, which I really enjoyed, and started wheelchair track in 1960. Since it was not an intercollegiate program, anyone who could push a wheelchair fast could participate, so, I did. I lost only one race in the next four-plus years and held what was called world records for my class in the hundred-yard and sixty-yard dashes.

My first coach was Kenneth "Casey" Clark, who later worked for the American Medical Association, and the U.S Olympic Committee, and became dean of the U of I College of Applied Life Studies. But in 1960 he was an assistant in athletics in the Rehab Services Division.

We raced in our fifty-pound chairs that we called "tanks." Now there are fourteen-pound chairs. Wonder how they keep them from taking off? Our longest race was a hundred yards, because anything longer supposedly would create an adverse reaction to our health. Quadriplegics now push in marathons, and the attitude about how much people with disabilities can exercise and stress themselves has changed greatly.

7

Wheelchair Safari Invades South Africa

An almost-free, once-in-a lifetime trip overseas beckoned in the fall of 1961. University of Illinois Rehabilitation Services Director Tim Nugent was putting together a six-week tour to South Africa and asked if Louise and I would be interested. Certainly!

The Wheelchair Safari was organized to demonstrate the skills of people with disabilities to a country that was not very involved in rehabilitation techniques. The entire tour was arranged and most of the money was raised by Tom Knowles, who was paralyzed from the waist down in 1952 in the crash of an English fighter jet. Knowles used a wheelchair and lived in South Africa, where he owned a travel agency. Louise graduated in the spring of 1961, and we joined a group of seventeen people with disabilities and nine who were able-bodied, departing for South Africa in June of 1962. There was great concern that so many people with disabilities would be flying as a group, and Nugent told me one airline kicked us off, apparently fearing the liability. Alitalia finally agreed to take us from New York to London, our first stop.

London brought us an unusual experience. Nurses, whom I think were part of the English Red Cross, were so concerned about our wellbeing that they told us we had to be taken to a hospital for an examination. After much negotiation, the 'ladies of mercy' allowed us to skip the hospital exams and continue on our way.

The next stop, in Rome, was scheduled to be twelve hours, and all of us were anxious for some rest. I can't sleep on a plane, and looked forward to a hot shower and a soft bed. As it turned out, that bed was a few hours away. Hosts met us at the airport and put us on a bus to show us the city. We saw some of the sites we had heard about all of our lives, though it was hard to keep our eyes open. I remember the Coliseum, the seven hills and the fountain made famous in the movie, "Three Coins in a Fountain." Not much else remains in my memory bank. The hotel room did not have a shower, and I had to settle for the tub. I can't remember if I ever got to that soft bed, because after we cleaned up our hosts fed us a big Italian meal. I was exhausted, but I speak only for myself, because some of the others on this trip seemed to have boundless energy.

As we flew into Johannesburg we learned that to save money, Tom Knowles had arranged for our group to split up and stay with families in their homes. All of the families were white. We talked well into the nights, telling each other about our lives and discussing the apartheid situation in South Africa. Many host families told us the racial and political situation in their country was terrible. They emphasized that they had to be very guarded with their comments out of fear about what their own government might do to them.

One of our tour members was Roger Ebert, now an award-winning film critic and author of the foreword of this book. A sophomore at the U of I, he was the South Africa tour reporter, sending stories about the trip back to Champaign-Urbana newspapers.

South Africa had few advanced rehab techniques at that time, and that is why Knowles arranged our tour. The government philosophy seemed to be that unless you had a healthy body, you were not much good to society. Knowles told us the South African national government was not enthusiastic about our visit and did not provide him money, transportation or encouragement. But on the local level we were celebrities everywhere we went. Mayors and other officials greeted us in Johannesburg, Durban, Cape Town and elsewhere. As we made speeches or gave demonstrations, we were front-page news.

Most of us ate too much of the most elaborate meals I have ever seen. Every host group tried to outdo the previous one. Most of our ground transportation was in small, vans. We saw mine dances, performed by workers at gold mines, and I have vivid memories of one dancer who had a wooden leg. We did skip an area that was reputed to have headhunters.

We played a basketball game in an ice arena on the second floor of a building. All of us who used wheelchairs had to be pulled up the steps. I was asked to speak to a boy who was twelve or thirteen and had talked about suicide because of his disability. He seemed to pep up while he watched us play basketball. After I returned home I was told the boy had changed his attitude completely and had started to participate in various kinds of sports. That alone made the trip worthwhile.

On another occasion we played basketball against a group of patients at a hospital for blacks. They used old-fashioned wooden wheelchairs with the big wheels on the front. However, it was a hard game because the baskets we were shooting at had no backboards. Try playing a game of basketball with just a hoop on a pole. The court was a dirt field, and bumpy. We won the game, but the score was close, something like 5-4.

We didn't see many other black groups but did meet several individual black youngsters with disabilities. Most were begging for money as they followed our group from place to place.

Louise is not athletically inclined, except as a spectator. On the trip she served as a cheerleader and also participated in our square dances.

Our tour was the beginning of a kind of revolution in South Africa for people with disabilities. We met with many medical professionals who saw what our group could do. We know from our long-time South African friends that there have been vast improvements in attitudes, rehabilitation techniques and equipment that allow better and easier movement of persons with disabilities.

As the South Africa tour was ending, Ian Smith's government in Rhodesia invited us to visit. His welcome was so much warmer than South Africa's that he provided a DC-3 and a pilot. The pilot was a jock who on one occasion tipped the plane's wings to say goodbye to our friends on the ground, and the cargo door popped open. We had to form a human chain to close it and did manage before we lost wheelchairs, luggage or people. The pilot also scattered herds of elephants, thinking we'd enjoy seeing them run.

One of the world's most remarkable feats of nature is Victoria Falls, many times bigger than our Niagara. We spent several hours marveling at its majesty and buying souvenirs from the natives who sold their wares around the falls.

I learned during the trip that despite a disability, you can participate in rigorous activities without hurting your health. We put in many eighteen-hour days and slept in rooms with little or no heat during South Africa's winter. I also learned that everyone on the trip was very much an individual, and that each reacted to various kinds of stress in different ways. All the individuals on the trip had different ways of dealing with their disabilities. They all knew what they could and could not do.

I was no exception. I once refused to sit in my wheelchair without the cushion. The chair and cushion had become separated in the vehicles used to transport our equipment. I refused to leave the van, which had a soft seat, until my cushion arrived. My refusal to budge held up the group, but as a paraplegic I have very thin skin on my buttocks and have had a few minor skin breakdowns over the years. Those breakdowns can take a few days to heal and I did not want a skin breakdown in the middle of a trip like this. I'm sure the whole thing seemed trivial to many of my companions, but to me it was necessary. So I stood my ground, or more accurately put, sat my ground, until the cushion showed up. Louise was angry at me for three days.

Nobody else, not even in the medical profession, should dictate to you. No one else knows just how far you can go and how much you can do. They have not lived in your body. One of the most important things one with a disability can learn is one's own strengths and weaknesses. My stubbornness grew from the knowledge that if I do something I shouldn't, I will put my system under undue stress. I've developed bladder inflections because of too little sleep, or perhaps I drank more alcohol than I should have had, and the plumbing system reacted negatively.

All of us on the trip also learned that being able to associate with a large group of people in a very close environment helps prepare you for the rest of your life. It allows you to deal with a diverse group of individuals. It was a six-week exercise in the development of personal relations. I grew up a lot. When the tour ended, I was a different person and a better person.

One disappointment was that Louise and I did not have the money to buy diamonds, which were priced very reasonably. I still owe Louise that diamond engagement ring.

Paul Luedtke, at that time an executive and part-owner of a moving and storage company, provided the expertise for our luggage and transportation needs, while Bob Wright, a retired military man who worked in the Rehabilitation Center, kept us organized, often saying, "Get with the program." Another friend, Henry Bowman, should have made the trip. He was the first black Big Ten football official, a retired military man and also an employee of the Rehab Center. Nugent wanted Bowman to go, but was told it would not be possible for an outside black to enter South Africa. How times have changed!

We returned via London to join the United States' wheelchair national team in competition at the international games. We had a few days to ourselves in London. The taxis were great, with room in the back seat for our wheelchairs to stand unfolded. But many cabbies were not anxious to pick us up. One day, we were invited to ride in a Bentley during a sightseeing tour with Lord and Lady Hamilton, friends of Tim Nugent. I was given, and smoked, a cigar from Winston Churchill's humidor at the Carleton Club.

Another day, we saw a large building with a guard stationed in front. I asked him the name of the building. He replied that it was Buckingham Palace. The others laughed at me, but at least I had the guts to ask. We were told that the boy waving from a window was four-year-old Prince Andrew.

Everyone in the group was propositioned in Soho. A lady who chatted with me unfortunately had a third-floor room. But even if the building had an elevator, I'm afraid Louise would have been very much against me using it.

Attending the games at Stoke-Mandeville near London was great because I could see what the British had accomplished in rehabilitation. Our tour organizer, Tom Knowles, had been in rehabilitation at Stoke-Mandeville after his crash. I am happy to report our U.S. team won the point total handily. I participated in several events, and still have the gold medal the team won in basketball.

Louise and I spent a grand total of $600 between us during the six-week tour.

I resumed work immediately when we returned home. Channel 3 had provided sixteen-millimeter black and white film and a camera for doing a show about the trip. I edited it for a thirty-minute program and was joined by Paul Luedtke who had taken hundreds of slides that we showed during the program.

We used the program to communicate to the viewing public the kinds of things we were trying to communicate in South Africa—that despite having a major physical disability, you can do what everybody else can do. You don't have to sit in Aunt Nelly's back room, in a nursing home, or in a hospital. You don't have to give up on life. The show received lots of good viewer comments. Afterward Paul and I hit the speaker circuit, because it seemed almost every group and organization in the Channel 3 viewing area asked us to appear. We took turns and tried to honor every request, making speeches and giving slide presentations on a regular basis for two or more years.

One disappointment after the trip was with Everest and Jennings Wheelchair Co., which claimed most of the U.S. market and opened a successful distributorship in South Africa after our trip. We had seen South Africans using the old wooden wheelchairs with big wheels in the front, like the chair that's associated with President Franklin Roosevelt. Everest and Jennings took advantage of the free publicity we gave them with the chairs we had purchased from their company and began selling them all over South Africa.

Tim Nugent had developed a good relationship with the company, which sponsored a yearly get-together for alumni and friends at the university. He told them our chairs took a beating during six weeks of being thrown on and off airplanes, buses and vans. Several were in very bad condition by the end of the tour. Tim told me the company responded with about $200 worth of free parts, perhaps enough to partially repair one or two chairs. Louise and I didn't see any of those parts. It would have been good public relations for Everest and Jennings to have repaired or even replaced our chairs. Unlike chairs today, they were solid pieces of equipment. The arms and the foot platforms were not adjustable and did not come off.

Despite our unhappiness with E and J, we continued to use their wheelchairs for many years. In fact, I bought a new one in 1965 and used it for thirty-three years. I also used the same cushion in my chair all that time. When the Illinois Central Railroad phased out steam engines and brought in diesels, the engineers and firemen no longer needed their eight-inch cushions made of stout rubber with large holes. My dad bought some of the cushions and we cut them in half, so I'd have a four-inch thick piece to sit on. We put plywood under the cushion to add firmness and covered it with Naugahyde. The rubber was so strong that it didn't mash down even a fraction of an inch.

I had to stop using the chair and the cushion a few years ago because of physical changes in my body. The fifty-pound chair I used so long cost $250. The wheelchair I bought in 1997 and use today cost $2,100. I bought a new cushion in 2000 for just under $600. Having a disability can be expensive.

Maxwell Leigh, South African journalist, whose family hosted Tom and Louise Jones for more than a week in the Cape Town area:
"The impression they made on us in their short stay has endured...Almost invariably when conversation with friends and new acquaintances turns to physical disablement we tend to talk about Tom and Louise and the example they set and continue to set...Tom was a typical and worthy representative of a team who presented to many similarly afflicted South Africans a demonstration of triumph of the human spirit over fettered bodies."

"Tom Knowles was paralyzed from the waist down in 1952 when at the age of 21 he crashed the Vampire jet aircraft of the Royal Air Force he was flying in England. And it was as a result of his subsequent experience at England's great rehabilitation establishment at Stoke Mandeville, headed by the legendary Dr. Ludwig Guttman (who was later knighted) and his observation of how much could be achieved in enabling the disabled to live fulfilling lives that Tom determined on his return to his own country, where so little was being done at the time or even thought of in this regard, to take positive action of his own."

"His dream has been realized many times over."

Tim Nugent, director emeritus of the Rehabilitation Education Center at the University of Illinois:
"In 1961 I was asked to send a representative group from the university to South Africa, Rhodesia, Upper and Lower Nyasland to demonstrate, educate and initiate activity in that part of the world on behalf of those with disabilities. It was decided to send alumni who had established themselves in their respective positions. This would be more meaningful. Just the introduction would tell a significant story. Tom and his wife, Louise, were among those chosen. He and his companions

did a superb job and many things now exist in those countries that would have been impossible otherwise. Many professional and lay people from South Africa have come to the University to study and to reunite with good friends."

Tour participant Paul Luedtke:
"This period was the introduction of Tom and Louise Jones into what would become a lifelong friendship, which I characterize as my closest friendship.

"…through some of the most enjoyable, exhilarating and in some cases trying circumstances, Tom Jones has demonstrated personal characteristics which are desired in many, but observed in very few people.

"These qualities led my wife and I (who have no siblings) to ask Tom and Louise to become the legal guardians of our children, in case of our demise."

8

They Really Pay Me to do This?

How would you like a job that allowed you to appear on television twice a day, be recognized almost everywhere you went within a hundred-mile radius of Champaign-Urbana, and talk and meet with many of the country's top entertainment, political, TV and radio sports personalities?

Some of the famous people I have met or interviewed are Roger Ebert, Bobby Knight, Woody Hayes, Jack Brickhouse, Pat O'Brien, Art Linkletter, Robert Goulet, Mrs. Babe Ruth, Arthur Ashe, Stan Musial, Enos Slaughter, Curt Flood, Warren Spahn, Whitey Herzog, Lou Brock, Tim McCarver, Lefty Gomez, Dizzy Dean, George Halas, Dan Deardorf, Jim Hart, Bob Hope, Tab Hunter, John Carradine, Susan St. James, Roger Miller, Harold Lloyd, Hans Conried, Arnold Palmer and Chi Chi Rodriguez.

I have worked with such good people as former Good Morning America weatherman John Coleman, St. Louis Cardinal broadcasters Mike Shannon and Bob Starr, and former Denver Cowboy and Texas Ranger broadcaster Mark Holtz. I met and/or interviewed some great U of I coaches, including Ray Eliot, Harry Combes and Lou Henson, and Illini athletes Red Grange, Lou Boudreau, Ray Nitschke, Jim Grabowski, Dike Eddleman and Gene Vance. I met every Illinois governor from William Stratton to Jim Edgar. I met and shook hands with Billy Graham. And they paid me to do this! I would have done it for nothing if I had some other way to make a living.

I learned what makes successful people different. Most were very nice. Only one or two were people I wouldn't want to go out and have dinner with.

My first sports program, Sunday Night Sports, was a big step because it primarily involved rewriting sports stories from the United Press International wire, covering university and high school athletics, interviewing a coach or a player. WCIA sports director Tom Schoendienst, a distant relative of former major league star Red Schoendienst, made many suggestions that helped me. He was sports director until 1971, when I took the job.

I did something that probably would not be recommended or even possible today. I worked full-time at Channel 3 during all of my junior and senior years in college. I worked at least forty and sometimes as many as sixty hours a week while carrying a full load of classes. I could do that because I went to summer school between my sophomore and junior years and again between the junior and senior years. That allowed me to lighten my load during the regular semesters. I missed a lot of things that the normal student would do, but working so much forced me to organize my time and probably made me a better student. I got the degree in four years, which many students are unable to do today. I remember eating Thanksgiving and Christmas dinners at the Walgreen drug store in Champaign, but it didn't bother me. Turkey and all the trimmings were available for a little over a dollar.

During one holiday break when the campus was almost deserted, I was pushing from my dorm to the Illini Union in the cold. At Huff Gym, a large fellow wearing only a short-sleeved shirt volunteered to push my wheelchair. He did, all the way to the Union, using only one hand and all the while walking beside me. I later learned that he was Ray Nitschke, who was drafted by the Green Bay Packers the next year. He played for the Packers for many years before being elected to the National Football Hall of Fame.

Graduation in the spring of 1959 brought me an offer of a regular full-time job at Channel 3. That meant I didn't have to send out resumes or audition tapes. What a relief! Not long afterward I was named chief announcer at the station. I knew if Channel 3 felt I had enough ability to give me the job, I'd been accepted for my talent. The fact I was in a wheelchair made no difference to anybody. Of course it shouldn't have, but remember that persons with severe disabilities were not much involved in the mainstream work arena in 1959.

The station had many interesting personalities. The weatherman, Wyndham 'Jack' Roberts and known as Mr. Roberts, was one of the kindest, gentlest, nicest men you'll ever want to meet. He didn't have the official designation, but he knew more about weather, weather systems and water systems than any trained meteorologist. So often the person you see on the air is not the person others know off the air. However, with Mr. Roberts, what you saw on the air was the real person.

Once when Mr. Roberts was out for an operation I filled in for him for my first stint as a weatherman. Since weathermen stand up and I couldn't, I had to figure out how to function on the weather set. We found a couple of wooden soda cases and a swivel stool, stacked the cases on top of each other, then put the four-legged stool on top of the cases. The stool had a high back, providing something to lean against. I lifted myself from my wheelchair up to that high seat. I always said that if I was going to stand up I was going to be about six feet four. There I was!

When the program started the cameraman shot me from the waist up, so the viewers thought I was standing next to the weather map. Then the other camera would take a tight shot on the map of the nation. We had attached a handle to the corner of the frame that held the maps. As the close-up was taken I'd grab the handle and swivel the stool to the left, making it appear I was taking a step. I'd note the temperature and weather fronts with my pointer. When we went to a commercial we would slide the panel and expose the state of Illinois map. After the commercial, I would talk about what was happening in Illinois. Then, just before going to the local forecast, I'd push the handle and it appeared to the viewer that I was taking a step back to the right.

I was a substitute weatherman for at least a year from my precarious perch! I never fell from the stool, but apparently I didn't leave a great impression with all the viewers. Louise says she doesn't remember me doing the weather.

When I first joined Channel 3 the news director was Fred Sorenson whose son Eric later became producer of the CBS Evening News with Dan Rather, then ran CNBC.

As chief announcer and also promotional copywriter I had to fire an employee who went on to greater glory. Larry Woiwode was a student at the university and was hired to write promotional copy for me. He was invariably late with that copy, causing me to be late for dinner. I finally went to our production manager and said, "Something's got to be done." He replied, "Well, if it happens again, we'll just have to let him go." It did, the very next week.

Several years later Woiwode won a Faulkner Prize for fiction. A Christian writer, he has been the laureate of North Dakota. Apparently he just could not handle tight deadlines. Besides, writing a promo for "I Love Lucy" certainly is not prize-winning stuff.

While I was directing I once had a chronically late noon newsreader. I warned him one time I'd turn the camera on an empty set if he arrived late one more time. I followed through. He was still in the station lobby when he saw the news set appear on a TV set. He raced down the hall to the studio and was forced to read the first part of the newscast while out of breath. He was very unhappy with me, but was never late again. That fellow got a law degree and later became a judge. I made certain I stayed out of his county.

And then of course there was John Coleman, my former high school classmate. He was a 'jack of all trades.' He did most of the weather programs Mr.

Roberts didn't do. He also had the responsibility for a program called 'The Hop,' a Saturday afternoon dance show for teenagers. It was so popular that on Friday or Saturday nights Coleman would put on sock hops at high schools. After leaving Channel 3 he was the main weather anchor on a Chicago TV station and on ABC Television's Good Morning America for many years. The Weather Channel we see on cable television was Coleman's idea.

My sports reporting responsibilities increased. I did Saturday sports through football season, making for many seven-day weeks. During basketball season I did most of the sports programs when Tom Schoendienst was doing play-by-play. I also was his vacation relief. All this time I was chief announcer and responsible for all the audio tapes. Then I was assigned to read the noon news.

I was beginning to suffer more bladder infections. Again, I'm sure they were caused by stress and failure to drink as much liquid as I should. I remember working many times with a 102-degree fever. That was especially uncomfortable if I was on the air and sitting in the studio with hot lights.

And yet during my entire Channel 3 career I did not miss more than a week or two because of illness. I knew if I took some medication and drank a lot of water, I would be OK in a day or two. But I never identified my ailment to my colleagues. I did not want to admit I was vulnerable to such things as bladder infections.

I once fell and broke a bone in my leg while transferring from my wheelchair to another chair prior to doing an interview. I didn't miss work. I put on a tight wrap because I wasn't going to walk on that leg anyway. I've had about five broken bones in my legs, two from participation in sporting events. Though I never felt direct pain, my body did react and sometimes I ran a low-grade fever. I tried to eat right and get eight hours of sleep almost every night in order to maintain such a rigorous schedule.

In 1965 the station manager and program director asked me to do a live morning talk show from 7:30 to 8 o'clock. They told me, "It's going to be called SunUp. There will be no script. You will ad-lib the whole show." It was one of the early television talk shows, patterned after a program offered by another Midwest Television owned station, San Diego's KFMB. I had to do the news, weather and all the interviews. KFMB's SunUp had a weathergirl named Raquel Welch. I put in a request for her, but understand she had other things to do for the next few years.

Roger Young was my first SunUp producer. I lost track of him until several years ago when I was watching the Emmys on television. There was Roger Young in Hollywood, winning an Emmy for directing. He has had seven Emmy nominations for his series of programs on the Bible and won an Emmy for "The Bible: Joseph."

For Sunup, I started work at 4:30 or 5 o'clock., and many times had to barrel my wheelchair, doing a wheelie by holding the front wheels up in the air, through fresh snow to get into the station. Many times I was able to negotiate snow almost a foot deep. Sadly, I can no longer do that.

The Sullivan Little Theater, about fifty miles south of Champaign, features stars every summer. A number of them appeared on SunUp. One was Pat O'Brien, who had acted in Hollywood movies for many years and must have been in his late sixties or seventies when I interviewed him. He showed up on time despite being up late to perform on stage the night before.

I asked him, "Why would somebody who's excelled in television, radio and the movies come to Sullivan in the middle of summer to do a show when you could be in your California home overlooking the ocean and resting?" He replied, "I do it to keep the tools sharp."

If you apply those few words, his philosophy of life, to whatever you're doing in your life, despite the problems you face, despite the odds against you, despite whether there's an easier road to take to reach your goals, you will be a success. I haven't always been able to do that, but I have tried to live my life that way.

Tennis player Arthur Ashe and I met under unusual circumstances. We checked into a motel at the same time while on fishing trips. I asked Ashe about the best fishing spots, but he was reluctant to tell me. Typical fisherman. I was driving to our fishing location. He had taken a private jet.

Hans Conried came to the U of I Assembly Hall for a show. He played a character on the old Danny Thomas TV show, and I thought an interview with him would be worth the whole thirty minutes, so had not arranged another guest. Toward the end of the show, when I started asking him about cooking and recipes, his comment was: "What's the matter? Are you running out of questions?" In fact, I had read something in his biography about his interest in cooking, and that's why I brought it up.

The show lasted five years and attracted many fans, including my dad who lived almost 200 miles from Champaign. He returned home from his railroad job in time to see the beginning of SunUp before a station in Harrisburg came on the air and blocked it. A sixty-foot TV antenna on top of our home in Carbondale allowed him to pick up WCIA.

I conducted a lot of out-of-station interviews and reports for SunUp. One person I interviewed was Roger Miller, who sang 'King of the Road.' My photographer, Bob Christianson, and I went to Mattoon to interview Miller. When we arrived, we found the interview had to take place on the third floor of a building. So Christianson, who was big and strong, took the camera upstairs. Then he pulled my chair up the three flights. Bob never complained. We got a very good interview, although I felt Miller was a little crazy.

Dizzy Dean did a wonderful interview. Toward the end, I asked him if he would sing his rendition of 'Wabash Cannonball.' He repositioned his big, white cowboy hat, thrust his head back and let loose with at least thirty seconds of the song. After his death I was told the station sent a copy of his singing to the network and it was used in the obituary on the CBS Evening News.

SunUp went to the State Fair for a week. One day at the fair is more than enough for me, but this was a whole week! We shared a stage used by Chicago radio station WGN for its farm show. There I was, for the whole world to see, sitting in my wheelchair on the stage and doing interviews. The cat was out of the bag. No longer was I required to transfer to a regular chair when I was on television. While at the fair I interviewed Bob Hope, whose answers were all one-liners, each one funnier than the last. He had flown in on what was then Ozark Airlines, and joked about the service, or lack of it.

Around that time I stopped the practice of leaving my wheelchair while reading news or sports at the station. Ten years had passed and attitudes toward persons with disabilities had changed. I hope I had just a small part in that change. But then there were still many, like a woman I met in a grocery store, who asked, "What happened to you?" I replied, "What do you mean?" She responded, "Well, I just saw you on television and you were perfectly fine. Now you're in a wheelchair." I explained that I had been in a wheelchair since I was six. She had watched me for years, unaware of my wheelchair. In her mind, if you use a wheelchair you can't be "perfectly fine."

Mrs. Babe Ruth gave me an interview while she was in Mattoon for the Babe Ruth Baseball League national tournament. I enjoy being able to say that while I didn't interview the baseball great himself, who died while I was a child, I did interview his widow.

As SunUp began, I started work on a master's degree in communications at the U of I. The director of broadcasting at the university arranged for me to take one class a semester while continuing to work full-time. I also accepted a teaching job in the college, instructing juniors and seniors in one or two classes each semester.

In 1969 I was named host of a program called 'Dialing for Dollars,' an afternoon show that offered money to people we called in the viewing area. If they were watching and knew how much we were giving away that day, they were winners. Amazingly, we paid a winner about once a week.

Several years ago, I encountered a woman at a Champaign shopping center who told me she used to watch me on Dialing for Dollars when she was in grade school. She was proud to tell me that now she was a grandmother. Talk about making a guy feel old.

Combining weekend sports with being the chief announcer, some directing, the early show and SunUp, working on a master's and teaching a university class or two, I had a full plate.

SunUp ended in 1970 while we were fishing in Canada. I remember telling the viewers that I'd be away for a couple of weeks and would talk with them when I got back. When I returned, there was no show. Management had taken it off the air without discussing it with me, indicating it had lost its impact on viewers or that the station wanted to telecast a network show at the time. I disagreed, but I worked for them. It was an inexpensive show to produce and because of all the mail we received each week I did not think the viewers had lost interest. I've tried to live by the words of an unknown author I ran across many years ago: "Accept your part and play it well, for therein all honor lies." Management said the show had run its course, and I had to accept the decision.

One event in 1970 relieved some of my disappointment in no longer having the morning program. The State of Illinois Division of Vocational Rehabilitation, as it was called at that time, named me "The Rehabilitant of the Half Century" in the state. What pleased me most was that my mom and dad were able to attend the presentation ceremony in Springfield, presided over by Gov. Richard Ogilvie.

I no longer rose at 4:30 in the morning, but I still had plenty to do, and within a year I became the WCIA sports director.

Tom Schoendienst took a TV job in Phoenix. A national search for a successor concluded with the job being offered to me. I wasn't sure I wanted the responsibility of two sports shows a day, six days a week, considering all my other duties. But on the other hand, it was a job I would give my right arm to have. It was one of the plum jobs in area television. One of the applicants was Jim Durham, who later broadcast Chicago Bulls games on television and now does a lot of free-lance sports on TV.

I had many questions before accepting. How would my health react? Would I have more bladder infections? Accessibility? What about getting in and out of press boxes? How am I going to cover Illinois football and basketball games at other schools? On and off airplanes? On and off buses? Traveling with the teams? Staying at hotels?

And my ability to announce? I'd never done play-by-play on TV and I'd never announced football. Did I have the skills? I had a pretty big ego and still do. I had enough confidence to know I could do the job. The wheelchair was necessary to get me from point A to point B, but wasn't going to keep me from doing my job.

The bottom line was that August C. Meyer Sr., owner of the station, wanted me to take the job. I quit doing 'Dialing for Dollars' and gave up the chief announcer's job. The station knew I sincerely wanted the sports job because I accepted the large raise of $10 a week to take on the responsibility.

Think about the change that had occurred in management since I started working there fourteen years earlier. Now they thought of me first as a television personality rather than a person with a disability. Of course that is what people with disabilities fight for today.

I've always believed that when the next opportunity comes along, you should say "yes" if you feel you are ready for the challenge. The only time I can remember thinking seriously about not accepting an offer was after this request to become sports director. As it turned out, I'm glad I didn't let worries about accessibility prevent me from accepting. It was a very hard, challenging job, but I would not trade that experience for millions of dollars.

The only other issues about my appearance were my bow ties, which I had worn since high school, and my receding hairline. On the advice of management, I bought a couple of straight ties and learned how to tie them. It was also suggested that I might look into toupees. But when I learned Frank Sinatra spent more than $1,000 on each of his toupees, I asked the station to pick up the tab. I never heard another word about my thinning hair and have never worn a hairpiece.

> *Carl Caldwell, co-worker at Channel 3:*
> *"Until I worked with Tom, I had never interacted professionally with a person in a wheelchair. From the very beginning of our relationship, Tom never made me feel uncomfortable about his disability, and I can honestly say that, within weeks of our initial meeting, I seldom noticed that Tom had a disability. I was simply not conscious of it because he is such a determined, strong-willed and confident individual."*

9

TV Sports Director on Wheels

For several reasons I anguished about putting my name in the hat to be considered for the sports director's job. One was that I would replace a man who was extremely popular with the viewers. Tom Schoendienst had been in the viewers' homes for 14 years. He knew what he was talking about, and could cram more sports into a three-minute program than anyone I have heard. He was not controversial. He did not offer opinions. He was the true sports fan's reporter.

When I took the job management told me they didn't care what the viewers had to say about me as long as they said something. I was told, "We really don't care if they criticize you or praise you, but we want them to talk about you." So one of my challenges was to put controversy into the sports reporting.

I did two sportscasts a day, six days a week, did play-by-play of U of I basketball on television, and color of football games on radio station WMBD in Peoria, also owned by Midwest. Management also wanted more coverage of high school and community college sports, as well as more in-depth coverage of smaller universities and colleges in the 100-mile circle Channel 3 covered. I wrote my own copy, developed my own interviews, produced my own programs. This was before much videotape, so when I had film I did most of the editing.

One of my favorite stories from my sports director years happened shortly after I took the job. The university wanted to change athletic directors and conducted a nationwide search. We arranged with the director of the U of I Public Information Office for a one-day notice before the selection was made public. We needed at least a 24-hour lead to be able to travel to interview the person who got the job and then return to Champaign.

When we got the call that the choice was Cecil Coleman, athletic director at Wichita State University in Kansas, it was time to fly. Photographer Bob Christianson and I left Champaign before daylight in a small plane and flew to Wichita to interview Coleman. Channel 3 was repairing or changing its film processor, so we landed near St. Louis to have the interview processed, then flew back to

Champaign and arrived a short time before I was to go on the air with the six o'clock show.

I did a quick edit of the film, wrote a quick script and got it on the air. After the program I edited a piece of the interview for our sister station in Peoria, WMBD, and sent it to them on our microwave relay system. Then I edited another piece for the ten o'clock show, wrote a new script and did that show. I returned home around midnight, after a day that began at three or four in the morning. It was certainly not a typical day, but it proved I could succeed at whatever came my way in the days and years ahead.

Cecil Coleman was the first athletic director who recognized efforts of the wheelchair athletes at the University of Illinois and saw that they received varsity letters. He let the National Wheelchair Basketball Tournament championship be played in the Assembly Hall. Channel 3 videotaped it and I did the play-by-play.

A couple of years after he became AD, Coleman offered me a half-time job doing radio and television relations for the athletic department. Fortunately, I turned it down to stay at Channel 3 because the annual pay would have been just over $8,000 and I didn't think that was enough.

The first color man I had on U of I TV basketball telecasts was Jim Wright, a former Illini basketball player. For the remaining years my color man was Gene Vance, a member of the Whiz Kids team in the 1940s. Given his long association with U of I athletic teams, Vance was very outspoken during the broadcasts. During a broadcast at Indiana his comments about officials became so loud that we were threatened with eviction from the arena. What great headlines that would have made the next day.

For football on radio, I did the color and Mark Holtz of WMBD did the play-by-play. It worked well because Holtz was talented at play-by-play and I had the color at my fingertips from being in town all week, talking with coaches, visiting with the players and watching practices.

Some road trips were unusually interesting. Once during a trip to Iowa City our small plane was freezing cold because air entered through a door that wasn't properly shut. The pilot put the plane down at an unattended airstrip near Pekin, got out, discovered the problem and slammed the door. Then he couldn't get back in the plane. He had locked himself out. Producer Larry Waters, who had an artificial leg below one knee, eventually hit the door so hard with his leg that it popped open. The pilot begged us not to tell his boss.

We once flew home from Columbus, Ohio, in fog so dense the pilot decided to land at a small airfield north of Urbana rather than the university's Willard Airport. I had to call Louise and get her out of bed to pick me up and take me to

Willard so I could retrieve my car. A second plane carrying the rest of the basketball players didn't leave Columbus until the next day. Illini coach Harv Schmidt was not happy.

I had to get on and off the planes. Though I am sure they would have been happy to help, I did not want to ask the players to carry me aboard. I'm sure they were capable, since I weighed only 135 pounds, but didn't want to see headlines the next day to the effect: "Football player can't play, gets hernia lifting sports broadcaster."

The solution was to shinny up the steps on my backside, then lift my body into the first seat. Today most airports have mechanical devices to assist passengers who can't walk, but I didn't know of any at that time.

Getting into and out of press boxes was not easy. Many were in older arenas or stadiums, in places we called "the catbird seat," way up high. You had to climb bleachers or steps. For basketball games my producer asked for special seating arrangements. All the athletic departments were accommodating, and at places like Iowa, Wisconsin, Michigan State and Northwestern I was seated on the floor, usually at the corner of the basketball court. Many times players or referees blocked my view to the point I'd need to check a TV monitor to see what had happened. Even so, I was able to do my job.

At Ohio State the radio broadcasting area for football was straight up a ladder. I climbed hand over hand, my legs trailing, before friends hauled up my wheelchair. Iowa's area was the most accessible—it even provided a restroom across the hall from where I announced. I sent George Wine, the sports information director, an award for providing the most wheelchair accessible press box in the Big 10.

The Illini football press box was reached by an elevator that stopped one flight of steps shy of the radio broadcast area. Dave Shaul, long-time Channel 3 news director and good friend, often pulled my chair up that flight. For post-game interviews with Illini basketball coach Harv Schmidt, someone would bounce my wheelchair down from the play-by-play area in the Assembly Hall to the playing floor so I could roar through a tunnel to the interview room. I was never late.

I had what I guess I would call a checkered announcing career in basketball. Schmidt's teams had started to go downhill. In the 1968–69 season his teams won nineteen and lost five, and he was hailed as a savior. The next two years his teams recorded fifteen and nine and eleven and twelve. During my first two years the teams were good with identical fourteen-ten records. Then in 1973–74 the record was five-eighteen, and Harv was no longer a savior. One year we telecast nine games and the Illini lost every one. In 1974 Illinois brought in coach Gene

Bartow from Memphis State, who recorded eight-eighteen in his one year before he moved on to replace John Wooden at UCLA.

I once asked former Illini player Rick Schmidt about his experience playing for Bartow. Schmidt said Bartow was a superstar coach who had no superstars in Champaign. Bartow complained that Illini alumni did not treat him as well as those in Memphis who had built him a tennis court behind his home.

Coach Harv Schmidt's failure to recruit Doug Collins, a Benton, Ill., native who went on to star at Illinois State and the NBA, could have been one reason for his downfall. Schmidt recognized that Collins was outstanding, but forgot to name him on a list of players he'd like to see at Illinois. The NCAA then did not restrict coaches who wanted to tell the media who they were recruiting. The word was that Collins heard his name was not on the list, so decided to go to Illinois State. I interviewed Collins later and asked him why he did not attend the U of I. He had no comment. If Harv Schmidt had recruited a player of his quality, it might have helped attract other quality players, and the downhill slide might have been averted.

Coach Schmidt and I broadcast a weekly TV show, featuring highlights of the past week's game. I also did that show for one year with Bartow. On radio, football coach Bob Blackman and I did a show that ran just before the game was broadcast.

While teaching later in the College of Communications I heard stories from other instructors about being contacted by coaches to help keep their players eligible. It also happened to me. I had a couple of Schmidt's basketball players in my class. One was the starting center and not doing particularly well in class. Two assistant coaches called to invite me to lunch. I accepted the invitation, paid for my own meal and politely informed my friends—I did consider all coaches my friends—that the player would earn the grade I gave him and that I would never give a grade that wasn't earned. The player did pass, and stayed eligible.

One of Schmidt's players ran afoul of the law, and an administrator from that player's high school came to Champaign to criticize the coach's handling of the situation. That criticism found its way into the media, and I urged Schmidt to respond on his TV show. He refused and the rest is history.

Bob Blackman came to Illinois from the Ivy League with a reputation as an innovator. I enjoyed a wonderful relationship with Blackman, who walked with a slight limp due to having polio as a child, but many of his innovations did not work against Big Ten defenses.

Two of my favorite non-Illini coaches were Bobby Knight and Woody Hayes. Both were irrational at times, but were competitive and successful. The first time

I interviewed Hayes he picked up another reporter by the collar of his shirt and held him in the air with one hand while he objected to the questions. I had done some homework, and knew I'd have a better chance at getting Hayes, a student of history and Abe Lincoln, to answer my questions if I began by asking him something about history. Perhaps another reason I never had trouble with Hayes was that I directed him to a bathroom at a coaches meeting in Chicago. I always try to be helpful to my fellow man.

I may be one of a handful of reporters that Knight didn't ridicule. In 1972 or 73 I asked him how long he thought he could coach. "No more than five years," he replied, saying the strain was too much. About 1980 CBS hired him as an analyst when Indiana didn't make the tournament. I wrote to compliment him on the job he had done and to remind him that he'd expected to quit coaching several years earlier. He wrote back to thank me for the compliment, but did not mention leaving coaching. Of course he still is coaching, now at Texas Tech.

For many years I was a board member of Champaign's Developmental Services Center. In the late 1980s, Knight spoke at a dinner honoring volunteers of the center. Former coach Lee Cabutti, also at my urging a DSC board member, persuaded Knight to fly in for the dinner and waive his $7,000 fee. He talked without notes for about forty-five minutes. We sold 500 tickets and could have sold at least 100 more if our space had been larger. As it was, DSC made a profit of more than $20,000.

Broadcasting the state high school basketball tournament was another job the Channel 3 sports director performed, and one I had wanted since high school. Again I broadcast with Mark Holtz, and we took turns doing the play-by-play and color. One outstanding game involved the Dolton Thornridge team that starred Quinn Buckner before he went on to Indiana and the NBA.

Another unforgettable memory involves the almost-new Illinois Assembly Hall, such a radical design that psychic Jeanne Dixon predicted it would fall down. During one game Mark and I heard the sound of a big chunk of concrete that had fallen from the ceiling, landing on the floor about two feet from us. We reported on the air that the sky was indeed falling, then quickly went back to describing the game. Amazingly, we never heard official comments as to the cause.

One television announcing team at the state high school basketball tournament broadcasts was most unique. It consisted of Ed McMahon, Johnny Carson's long-time sidekick, Red Auerbach, former coach of the Boston Celtics and Ed McCauley, former college and NBA star. After all of us had finished our announcing duties they joined me at the TV station to look at videotape and produce highlights to be shown prior to the next day's telecast. Each had his own idea of what should be included, and it fell to an engineer and me to put the final product together. Needless to say, with all the different opinions it took what seemed like forever to finish the editing. I remember getting home about three in the morning, my whole being reeking from the smoke of Auerbach's famous cigar.

As I finished my fourth year as sports director I had started to become fatigued and became concerned that the stress of working six days a week would burn me out and harm me physically. I even went to management and asked if there was something else I might be able to do at the station. They couldn't come up with anything, so apparently it was either stay as sports director or go somewhere else. And someplace else fell into my lap.

The University of Illinois Office of Public Affairs wanted to start a major radio-TV unit and asked if I would take that public affairs job. It allowed me to continue to do similar work but in a different arena and with much less stress. I'd considered trying to move to a larger TV market, but my research for a master's degree showed me the negativism I would confront if I applied for jobs in larger cities. If I moved to a larger market I would compete with people who had a tremendous number of years of experience and who did not use wheelchairs to get around. This was 1974, when people in wheelchairs were not nearly as visible in the workplace as they are today.

Some of the responses to my master's research will explain what I mean. A top manager at a successful station responded to my survey by writing that people in wheelchairs should not be in the work environment—they should be in hospitals or nursing homes. His responses revealed that he had no experience with people who used wheelchairs. His opinion was based on total ignorance.

Other comments: "We have so much electrical equipment in the station I would be afraid they would be electrocuted." "It's hard enough for fully trained professionals who are totally ambulatory to get about in this business. A wheelchair patient? Impossible and totally unfair to him." "A person in a wheelchair could not handle the job without an assistant. It would be economically impractical for the station to consider hiring such a person."

Two other station managers voiced the same opinion as my TV station about showing the wheelchair on camera. "I would not show a handicapped person's wheelchair on camera because the viewer should be able to identify as fully as possible with the talent. Every handicapped person I've known has had fantastic emotional hang-ups. This is a problem I don't need."

And, finally: "I would not put such a person on the air at all. The wheelchair would tell the viewer we are trying to win an audience by putting this person on the air. I don't want the viewer to think we are looking for the sympathy vote."

I could give more examples, but it is painful to think that persons in charge of many of this country's top broadcast facilities were that stupid.

Another reason to remain in Champaign was Louise. She was ensconced in a full-time job she enjoyed in Admissions and Records at the U of I. We'd built a wonderful house, and enjoyed many friends and activities in Champaign-Urbana.

I gave up something I had a life-long desire to do when I made the move to public relations. It was one of the hardest decisions of my life. I tried to not look back, and have said I do not miss it. But if I had to do it again, I would. My last full-time appearance on Channel 3 came on Dec. 31, 1974. I continued as the back-up sportscaster for another year and a half, and also was the vacation relief for my successor, Don Wilcox, who had been my student in one of my broadcasting courses and had my wholehearted endorsement for the job.

The station owner, August C. Meyer, persuaded me to keep my hand in at the station. He said something to this effect: "Young man, we would like you to continue some kind of relationship with us because your profit-sharing is down. The market will go back up, and we would like you to have an opportunity to take more money out of the profit sharing." I replied, "That's probably a good idea."

By mid-1976 it became apparent my two jobs were in conflict. The public affairs office did not want their employees to work elsewhere and did not want other media in the area to think I gave Channel 3 preferential treatment. That wasn't happening, but I knew it was a perception. Also, technology at the station was passing me by. In addition, my profit sharing had increased because the stock market went up tremendously in that year and a half. By the way, Forbes magazine said Meyer was worth $400 million when he died. Here was a man who knew what he was talking about when it came to money.

I also had to give up the teaching position when I joined Public Affairs. I was told I couldn't have more than 100 percent employment at the university, so I would have had to teach for free. I said, "I think I've got enough irons in the fire, so I'm not going to volunteer to be a teacher."

I guess I didn't realize just how much fame I had gained in that hundred-mile circle around Champaign. Louise and I were driving through Arlington National Cemetery near Washington on one of our vacations when someone looked in the window of our car and said, "Oh, there's Tom Jones!" During one of our many fishing trips to Canada we had flown to a camp way out in the boondocks and were fishing on Rice Lake when a boat pulled up next to ours and a regular Channel Three viewer recognized me. It is, indeed, a small would.

Being recognized is nice, but the hardest part of giving up the TV job was leaving the daily relationships I had built up over the years. Several of those I worked with have continued to be very good friends, and I treasure them.

I met Larry Waters when he was a high school student in Arthur, Ill. He had injured the lower part of one leg in a football game and had to have it amputated. Larry and his father attended a practice session of the Champaign-Urbana Black Knights wheelchair basketball team, a community team of recent U of I graduates. We knew he'd be a terrific addition to our team because of his good balance in the wheelchair. But when his dad saw how rough wheelchair basketball was, he said, "No, we're not going allow him to play." Larry and I met again when he was about to graduate from Southern Illinois University at Carbondale and asked me about applying for a job at Channel 3. I put in a good word and he got the job. He produced many of my sports telecasts and broadcasts before I went to work at the university and he went on to another TV station.

Another good friend and former co-worker is Carl Caldwell, who came to Channel 3 before I left, having almost landed a job at WGN in Chicago. When I moved to the U of I, we hired Carl to help me with an expanding television component in the Office of Public Affairs. Carl is now in charge of WILL, the University of Illinois TV station.

Bob Blackman, former U of I football coach:
"I remember Tom for his big smile and his warm and friendly personality. Although you had to be aware that Tom was in a wheelchair, you very quickly forgot about the disability and never thought of him as a 'handicapped person.' If conducting an interview, Tom was always well prepared and very professional. He had a great knowledge of sports but could converse equally well on most any other subject."

Tom Schoendienst, co-worker Tom followed as Channel 3 sports director:
"Tom Jones had a very solid sports background and proved to be an excellent announcer during our years together at WCIA. But more significantly, he has a fine personality and is one of the most positive persons I have ever known."

Larry Waters, former co-worker at WCIA-TV:
"Tom shared a lot of insight with me and during my senior year of high school I occasionally talked to Tom to seek his advice...Turn the clock forward four years...I started my career as a broadcaster as a producer/director at WCIA in February, 1969, with Tom's advice and assistance."

10

In Search of the Big Ones

Our trip overseas whetted our appetites for travel. During our two-week summer vacations, Louise and I drove wherever we could. Here were two people in wheelchairs, venturing into uncharted territory. This was before the great emphasis on accessibility in motels, restaurants, bathrooms or public transportation. Most communities had few, if any, curb cuts. We had to take catch-as-catch-can and hope that when we got out of the car we were going to be able to get into the building at our destination.

Vacations were sometimes an experience we would rather not have had when we found places inaccessible. But when we look back on all the things we tried to do, and did successfully, we laugh and wonder how in the world we did it all. We took one trip to Lake of the Ozarks in the Missouri hills. We wanted to ride on a dinner boat, but as I looked down at the lake where the boat was docked, I saw what must have been 100 steps straight down. The people in charge did not hesitate. "No problem. We'll get you down there." They took each chair down the steps to the boat. When we finished the dinner cruise, they carried the chairs up again.

In addition to architectural barriers there were attitudinal problems. I am sad to say some of those problems still exist. It is very difficult to pass laws that prohibit attitudes. But in areas like Lake of the Ozarks in the Bible belt, we found that people couldn't do enough for us.

We also spent some vacations visiting family in Carbondale and Hinsdale. It was good to see them, but also good we lived more than 100 miles from each, because we wanted the world to know we could live on our own and didn't need constant help from family and friends. We proved we could!

My love of fishing resulted in many vacations in search of big ones. One early trip took place in 1965 with friends Chuck Dahncke and Wayne Broeren, both of whom also used wheelchairs. Wayne, who was a great help to us when we built our second house, had been fishing at one Wisconsin lake several times. It turned out to be a muskie lake. The muskie is one of the biggest, meanest, freshwater fish you can catch. The lures must weigh three pounds. Wayne said he'd cast at least 500 times a day and considered it a successful day if a muskie at least followed the lure to the boat. Muskie fisherman are happy just to see the fish. Charlie and I ended up catching a lot of rock bass that were small and wormy. But we had fun. So much fun that Chuck and I invited our wives, Louise and Adrianne, to join us on our next fishing trip, which was to Minnesota. Adrianne is able-bodied, the only one in our group.

My dad had ordered me to call as soon as we arrived. I didn't. A while later, out on the lake, we saw an airplane circling. When we returned to the dock the woman who ran the camp said I had received a phone call. My dad was on the other end of the line. He'd been so worried that he called the sheriff, who sent the search plane. Despite my dad's concern, the vacation was so good that the four of us planned more fishing trips.

After a lack of fishing luck in Wisconsin and Minnesota, in 1968 we decided to try Canada. We chose a camp in Sioux Lookout, Ontario, operated by a family named Anderson. Before we went we talked to them about what people in wheelchairs would need. They built a ramp or two for us to enter some of the buildings, and we fished there for several years.

When the Andersons sold that camp, we moved to Storke Lake, a fly-in camp near Red Lake, Ontario, where the fishing for walleye and northern was great. We would drive to Red Lake and hire a floatplane that took us to the camp. These same planes stocked the camps in winter, so the ramps used to roll barrels of oil into the planes were available to roll our wheelchairs into the passenger area. The camp's owner built ramps which allowed us to get into the cabins and even constructed a very long ramp that led to the dining facility, where we were treated to fantastic meals for breakfast and dinner.

Our guide once decided to take us on a long boat ride, about twenty miles from camp. Why is it that fishing is always better after a long boat ride? However, as darkness approached, the boat I was handling developed motor trouble many miles from the cabin. Fortunately, Norm, our guide, carried two motors on his boat. He managed to balance between the boats and swap the motors. Since I was piloting the second boat on an unfamiliar lake, it was remarkable that I avoided hitting some submerged rocks. We got back to camp around midnight. Freshly caught walleye was delicious even at one o'clock in the morning.

In the summer of 1974 I fished in the Northwest Territories. They told us it was about fifty miles from the Arctic Circle. Also on that trip, during the year President Nixon resigned, were Chuck Dahncke, Paul Luedtke and his son Eric.

After almost every cast we'd hook an eight-to-fifteen-pound trout that would dive straight down into several hundred feet of cold water. We had to release many fish after fighting them into the boat, because of government limits placed on how many you could bring home. It was the only time in my life I put down a fishing pole and said, "I'm just too tired to continue."

Once in the Northwest Territories the Eskimo guide in my boat saw one of the beautiful white wolves that roam the area and got ready to shoot it. I stopped him, an act that cost him a $200 bounty. I knew it wasn't a fair fight when I was shot, and I did not want the same thing to happen to this beautiful animal. I did give the guide a larger than average tip at the trip's conclusion.

In all our years of fishing in Canadian waters Louise was the best fisherman of the group. Her real skills are in jigging for walleye. She could out-fish everyone in the boat, including the guide. But she's allergic to fish. Since she can't touch the bait or the fish, every time she catches one somebody must remove it from the hook and put on new bait. She is so allergic to fish that it dangerous for her to eat them. We once encouraged her to try some fresh-caught fried walleye. She did and immediately began to develop symptoms, including a tightening in the throat. Fortunately, Adrienne carried an antihistamine and the crisis passed. We learned our lesson. I tell her that although she is technically a fisherman, she doesn't do half the stuff a fisherman has to do. I also tease her that she catches so much more than everybody else because everybody else is tending to her fish and her bait. Of course, she doesn't agree.

One of the first guides looked at me strangely and asked, "Have we met before?" I replied, "No, I don't think so." It turned out that Norm Snyder had been a pharmaceutical salesman who watched me on television while he lived in Springfield. He gave up that life to be a fishing guide in the summer and a hunting guide in the winter. Yes, it is a very small world.

In 1965 Louise started a new career at the U of I Office of Admissions and Records, and I began the SunUp program while working on my master's degree. I'm not sure why I wanted the master's, except I had time on my hands to take classes. We also built a new house in 1965, at 1205 Theodore Drive, Champaign, where we still live. Tim Nugent, who lived across the street, tipped us about the lot and we arranged a thirty-year loan at five percent interest. But we had to come up with a twenty percent down payment. I had been buying stocks since my junior year in college, so I sold several thousand dollars worth and Louise's mother lent us the rest, which we repaid with interest. That $32,500 house is valued at well over $100,000 today.

As I have already indicated, in 1968 I was asked to teach a few classes in the U of I College of Communications. I taught either quarter-time or half time for seven years, but wouldn't want to be a full-time teacher.

This was the era of the Vietnam War and the protests against it. One student activist looked like an unkempt Mark Spitz, the Olympic swimmer. At the end of the semester I told my student he would have to clean up his act to land a job in television. A few days later a Mark Spitz look-alike walked in the door at Channel 3 to apply for a job. The activist soon began work as a TV weatherman.

An attractive woman student in one of my classes moved to Chicago after graduation and wrote to say she had an opportunity to read news at a Chicago TV station. It was a new station and planned a midnight newscast with the newsreader in bed, I assume alone. She asked in her letter if I thought she should take the job. By return mail, I wrote, "Certainly, no matter what it takes to get in the door. You do it, because that might lead to something else." She was the first to read news in bed, and I consider her one of my successes.

Near the end of my master's program, in addition to the thesis, I prepared a video on my career. It was about twenty minutes long and titled, 'Big Wheel in Broadcasting.' It explored opportunities available for the persons who used wheelchairs in broadcasting. I surveyed about 600 radio and television stations across the country to learn how many people in wheelchairs worked in broadcasting as on-air personalities. I learned of four people in wheelchairs in radio and one in television. That one was me. A few station officials indicated they would hire someone in a wheelchair, but no such a person had applied. I am sure one of the reasons no one in a wheelchair applied for a job at his or her station was that people who used wheelchairs were not then encouraged to train for such a profession. Without the encouragement for proper training, there were few if any such applicants at broadcasting stations.

I finished the master's in 1971. That was the year our dog Sam passed away. We didn't want another dachshund, but did want another small dog that wouldn't mind being in the house a lot. We settled on a West Highland White Terrier. We looked at a litter one day, just to learn about the breed, and came home with Oscar.

My urologist at Carle Clinic told me in 1974 that I needed to have a 'super pubic' installed. Basically, a surgeon punches a hole through your abdomen and into your bladder, then inserts a tube that drains the urine so you have no residual buildups that can cause infection. While voiding, most paraplegics leave some urine in the bladder, and I know that's one reason I was developing infections. Tests showed the urine was not building up to the point it would back up and produce a much more severe infection or damage my kidneys. I told the urologist it was too big a step and I didn't want to live the rest of my life with a hole in my abdomen.

A while later I went to Washington, D.C., to speak at a rehabilitation conference. While there I networked with people to find the best urologist in the country—and coincidentally watched on television as President Nixon resigned a mile or so away. A doctor who was recommended was at the Indiana University Medical Center in Indianapolis.

Back home I phoned for an appointment with Dr. John Donohue. It was a life-changing visit. He said the super-pubic was not the solution, and gave me other options. He started me on massive doses of Vitamin C and changed the antibiotic I had been taking for several years as maintenance to one called Bactrim. My bladder infections were reduced from two or three a year to one a year.

But I was not satisfied, and two years later I returned to Donohue and he referred me to Dr. John Mulcahy, new on the Indiana staff after experience at the University of Kentucky and Mayo Clinic. Mulcahy suggested self-catherization, which my Carle doctor said would cause more problems than it would solve, because I would be introducing more germs into my bladder. But I opted for Mulcahy's approach. Since then I've performed self-catherization three or four times a day and have suffered no more than five or six infections with fever since the mid-1970s. And I do not have to drink eighteen glasses of water a day. Self-catherization draws all the urine from the bladder, leaving less chance for infections to develop. It proves that if you ask around and find the right people, you can find someone who can help. You must be your own advocate—and network. I can't emphasize enough how important it is for people with disabilities to network, whether looking for a job or a solution to a medical problem.

1974 turned out to be one of the saddest years Louise and I experienced in our marriage. Her brother died and my father passed away. My mother had been told to slow down or jeopardize her health. She had been working two jobs, at the SIU Carbondale health service and at home with my dad, who had Parkinson's disease. She made the difficult decision to move my dad to a nursing home. I am sure he gave up, because I remember him saying he would never live in a nursing home. When he was younger, many nursing homes were run by the county and were not nice places to be. Dad died a week after the move. My mother regained her own health in the next few months.

Looking back, I wish I had told my father that he played a major part in everything I have been able to do. He gave me drive. He taught me discipline and to work hard. And I would tell him I knew he loved me greatly and that I loved him equally. My mother also played a major part in helping to make me what I am today, as did my brother and many schoolmates.

I have already mentioned my friend, Dale Jones, who would go out of his way to help me participate in all the activities during our grade and high school years. It is with great fondness that I remember riding around in Dale's old red Chevy, looking for girls. Louise and I regularly get together with Dale and his wife Liz, who live just 40 miles away.

The fact that I was able to live a life that was pretty much the same as all my friends gave me the ability to survive as an independent person.

The full-time job at the U of I Office of Public Affairs paid $14,000 in 1975, $2,000 more a year to start than I was making at Channel 3 after 18 1/2 years. And it was basically a Monday-Friday daytime job, a more relaxed lifestyle.

One of my disappointments upon leaving television was not being able to possibly motivate other persons with disabilities who might be watching me. I'll give you an example.

Louise hired a young woman named Barb to work with her at the university. During a conversation, Barb told Louise that I was her hero. She related how as a child with polio who was very dissatisfied with her life she used to watch me on television. When she discovered I used a wheelchair, her attitude became positive. She thought if someone in a wheelchair could work on television, she could do anything she wanted to.

Many people wonder why I would give up the glamorous position on television. I always reply that television is much more glamorous to those who watch it than to those who produce it.

11

Two More Jobs and Willie Nelson

When I went to work at the U of I, I felt that I was giving back something to the great institution that had been so important to Louise and me. The U of I made higher education possible for many hundreds of people who have disabilities.

I had the opportunity in my job to enhance the university's image. As director of Broadcast Services in 1975 I began developing extensive television feature presentations. Many of the videos were shown during half-time breaks on basketball and football telecasts. At the same time I provided radio stations with stories about the university. I developed a successful statewide radio network, offering audio tape stories about the university on a telephone line Monday through Friday.

I called the Associated Press and United Press International in Chicago early every morning and provided them with details about the story available. In turn, they informed all the stations in Illinois and many in surrounding states about the stories. I interviewed people on campus about subjects in the news and tried to give stations new features to be used almost immediately. I put new stories on the phone line at nine and three-thirty each day and it was not uncommon for each story to receive thirty to seventy calls. It was a great opportunity for the university's name to be heard in several states, and it told the taxpayers of the wonderful things happening at the U of I.

About 1980 I was named associate director of the Office of Public Affairs, in addition to being director of broadcast services. It allowed me to develop good working relationships with two U of I presidents, John Corbally and Stanley Ikenberry. I helped President Ikenberry produce his State of the University television message that was then distributed to stations around the state.

University of Illinois professors were in demand around the country to provide expertise on current hot topics in the news. I would occasionally accompany them on trips to major radio stations when they appeared for in-studio interviews. Flying was quite an experience, and one trip is emblazoned in my memory.

For a flying trip from Champaign to St. Louis in a seventeen-seat 'puddle jumper' for an appearance on KMOX radio, I had to use my normal method of getting into the plane—pulling my body, one step at a time, into the cabin section and then using arm power to lift into a seat. When the elderly pilot saw what I had to do to get on the plane he refused to take off, saying I was a danger to all others on board. The trip was saved when a younger pilot intervened by indicating he had seen how mobile and strong I was and that I would not impede access to the door by other passengers. Other flights since then have produced better results, but I am told by regular fliers that persons with disabilities often still face major problems.

Some directors of public affairs didn't understand the difference between true news stories and public relations plugs. One of my bosses, Fred Mohn, was a former United Press International staffer, and we seemed to speak the same language. But not all did.

One reason I left the public affairs job was a dispute with one of the office's directors about the difference between media relations and public relations. Having worked in the commercial media I knew what stations would use and what they would not.

My last duty in Public Affairs in 1985 was to assist in the first-ever Willie Nelson Farm Aid, which was held in the U of I's Memorial Stadium. We counted 1,300 media people from all over the world. I was so busy that I did not see Willie, but I did see his fancy bus.

For the International Year of Disabled Persons in 1981 I was the local chairperson. Mayors of Champaign and Urbana and the chancellor of the university named me to the post. My job was to organize and work with individuals and groups on programs that would call attention to situations faced by people with disabilities and then remedy them. A major project was to build an accessible playground in Champaign. It gained broad attention with a nationally distributed promotional message for television. We also worked with real estate people to set up a listing of accessible apartments and homes. I visited children to talk about what it is like to use a wheelchair, and some enjoyed riding on my lap. I probably made twenty or thirty of those appearances, and hope they made a lasting impression. Since then, several of our projects were taken over by other groups or service clubs. The university allowed me time away from my regular duties when I needed to work on an IYDP project.

The university in 1983 hosted a summer athletic competition called the Prairie State Games, opportunities for high school, college and older athletes to be involved in good competition during the summer months. The games still exist at other sites, but are nowhere as big as when the U of I was the host.

Getting the games publicized and the results to the news media were headaches. The U of I, merely the host, was being criticized by some media sources for doing a poor job for them. After the first year, politicians came from the Illinois Legislature to Champaign to ask for the loan of a media director for several months, to work before the start of competition and during the games. Since the state was contributing a large amount of money to make the games work, they did not want the U of I to continue receiving unfair criticism. One of those state legislators was Dennis Hastert, who went on to become Speaker of the House in Washington.

University officials came to me and said, "We would like for you to set up a system whereby the results would be disseminated in a proper, efficient and accurate fashion." They added, "You're going to be relieved of some of your regular duties to be able to do this job."

From experience I knew that I was agreeing to take on a second full-time job for a few months of the year. I hired twenty-five or thirty communications students, gave them a two-day training session, negotiated with computer companies and set up a pressroom. From January through midsummer for the next three years I was on loan to the Prairie State Games. The amount of time required was overwhelming. The first year was rough because none of us knew what we were doing. But the second and third years were outstandingly successful.

One true joy in working on the Prairie State Games was to get to know Hall of Fame broadcaster Jack Brickhouse, who was master of ceremonies during the three years I was involved. I prepared the script that Brickhouse used during opening and closing ceremonies. During one of our script-preparation meetings in a hotel bar a young couple approached us. It seemed obvious that the couple recognized Jack and wanted to meet him. We were both surprised when they directed their comments to me and asked if I had appeared on television in Champaign. When I replied that I had, they said they used to watch me. Then, looking straight at Brickhouse, they asked, "Is that Harry Caray?" Without missing a beat, Jack replied, "No, I am his illegitimate son."

I also volunteered to help the Mental Health Department, taking phone calls from people considering suicide and trying to persuade them to seek professional help. Since I worked during the day, my shift was from eleven at night until seven in the morning. I remember many sad conversations with some very desperate people. I have always felt it is important to help others less fortunate by getting involved with volunteer work.

I have also been involved with the U of I Division of Intercollegiate Athletics in several areas. After leaving Channel 3, I broadcast play-by-play of several Illini men's games on WILL-TV. I also was public address announcer for women's basketball games and for one season announced play-by-play on radio for the women's games.

In the mid-1980s our next-door neighbor, Floyd "Gordie" Gordon, suggested that we join forces and buy some kind of business. I mentioned that my cousin Bill Crenshaw had opened a Baskin-Robbins ice cream store in Carbondale and had been so successful that he was moved to the main office in Burbank, Calif. Gordie was interested, so I contacted Bill. We passed muster with a company official responsible for authorizing the sale of existing stores, and we bought a store only half a mile from home.

The store was owned by Lou Henson, the U of I basketball coach, and his wife, Mary. Their three daughters also worked in the business, which we learned later was a great advantage. Those young ladies provided the Hensons with loyal, properly trained ice cream dippers. On several occasions we saw some of our own employees over-dipping for their friends.

Gordie and I attended the company school in California to learn how to do things the Baskin-Robbins way. Back at home it quickly became apparent that the business was too small for two decision-makers. Though we had a verbal agreement about our roles, sometimes we forgot. Louise and I had bought the store as a moneymaking project, not as a working project. So Gordie agreed that the partnership was not working. Since we didn't want the store to ruin our friendship, I offered to sell our half to the Gordons, to which they agreed.

I'd been a businessman for less than a year. It was nice to have had the experience, but never again!

We still traveled often and great distances to Phoenix, Ariz., Jackson Hole, Wyo., the Grand Tetons, Victoria Island in Canada, the Black Hills, back to California and to the state of New York. Chuck and Adrienne Dahncke were our frequent traveling partners. There we were, three people in wheelchairs, filled with the spirit of adventure though we did not know what kinds of accessibility we would find. Even today, we find that what someone thinks is accessible is occasionally only marginally so.

I cannot tell you how many times we have been assured by motels and hotels that they offer what is called a 'wheelchair accessible' room. However, after checking in, it turns out to be a different story. One hotel presented three steps—just to get to the front door. One narrow bathroom door forced us to transfer from a wheelchair to a folding chair and literally scoot across the floor to reach the toilet.

At about the same time the Dahnckes discovered a winter vacation spot in New Smyrna Beach, Fla., about twenty miles south of Daytona. The Golden Arms, a condominium development the owners rent to visitors most of the year, became the regular winter destination for both families. It was totally accessible, with good parking, a ground-level entrance, an elevator to every floor and plenty of room.

We sipped our morning coffee on the balcony over looking the Atlantic Ocean each day. Then we drove to a good spot on the beach with a cooler of pop or beer. The sand was so fine and tightly packed that we could push our wheelchairs on it. We drove to Disney World and to Marathon Key. One year, just as our vacation was ending, we decided to see the sun come up over the Atlantic and set over the Gulf. We watched the sunrise on our balcony, then drove across the state to St. Petersburg to see the sunset. We made it with about 10 minutes to spare. Louise's shopping adventures during the trip almost caused us to be late.

My mother married again in 1977. Her new husband was Dennis Hays, a long-time resident of Carbondale. They enjoyed each other and did many things together for a couple of years. Then my mother began developing severe headaches, and one morning, Dennis could not wake her. Doctors at Carbondale Hospital sent her to Barnes Hospital in St. Louis, where they discovered a brain tumor. Surgery followed, allowing her limited functioning.

On the Fourth of July in 1980 Dennis phoned to say she was failing. She died the same day, liberated from her living hell on Independence Day. She died at seventy, the same age as my dad when he died. My mother was not the taskmaster my father was. Yet, because she was a professional nurse, she was able to do things for me in my early years that allowed me to be as healthy as I am today. Though I sometimes rebelled against her advice, it in no way diminished our love for each other.

The stress of my mother's death and my position as associate director of public affairs may be what caused severe pains in my back. The brace I had worn for many years was causing a lot of pain in its upper contacts with my body. Over the years the curvature of my spine had become worse, requiring the brace to be tightened repeatedly. Dr. Jim Harms at Carle Hospital in Urbana recommended surgery to insert metal rods in my back. Harms had never performed the surgery on a paraplegic, so I asked for the name of another surgeon. He referred me to

Dr. Paul Meyer at Northwestern University Hospital in Chicago. When I met with Meyer he agreed a hundred percent with Harms. Two years later, when the pain became almost unbearable, I decided to go ahead with the surgery.

Harms said the procedure would require two surgeries. He would take vertebrae out of the spine, remove a rib, chop the rib into small pieces and place the pieces in the spine where the vertebrae had been. Rods about the length of a small pen then would be wired and screwed up and down the spinal column.

Surgeries were performed two weeks apart. When Harms announced it was time for the second operation, I said, "You have to be kidding; I'm dying from this pain." He assured me I would survive. The ninety-degree curve was straightened to twenty-eight degrees. I spent a month in the hospital, then wore a large plastic brace for six months. Harms wanted me to wear the brace day and night, but I talked him out of it. I promised never to turn during the night while it was off. This is another case of being a self-advocate. It spared me skin breakdowns, which would have occurred had I worn the brace fulltime. After six months the bone encompassed the rods and gave me solid support in my back. Though I returned to work in three months, it took me well over a year to regain my strength.

I haven't had to wear a heavy back brace since then. However, some curvature has developed below the last rod and begun causing me difficulty. I talked with Harms about doing more work, but he is reluctant.

In 1985 I was given the opportunity to move to a job in the Division of Rehabilitation Services as assistant director for special events. I was in charge of community relations, alumni relations, media relations, fundraising and other things. It put me closer in touch with the more than 1,500 people with disabilities who are alumni of the more than fifty-year-old rehabilitation program. I performed a variety of productive services using training I had acquired in commercial television, university public relations, university teaching and public speaking.

Joe Larsen, a former director of the U of I School of Life Sciences and a longtime wheelchair user, had succeeded Tim Nugent as director of the division. He was a religious man and very kind to me as I learned new and expanded responsibilities of the job.

One of the great pluses was the opportunity to work with Joe Konitzki, a former AAA baseball player in the Giants organization at Minneapolis. I had known him since he joined the division in 1962. Konitzki is one of the finest individuals I have known and remains a good friend. I also became involved in Sigma Signs, the annual publication of Delta Sigma Omicron, a service organization for students with disabilities.

Director Larsen asked me to make the Sigma Signs publication more informative and readable while keeping the division's name in the forefront of all such units in the country that were beginning to offer services to college students with disabilities. I recruited advanced magazine students to help, added color and asked former students to help pay for the additional cost. In a year we tripled the amount of contributions. When I retired in 1991 Sigma Signs had $10,000 in the bank.

Larsen also asked me to establish a job placement conference. He had found that many students with disabilities never arrived at the interview stage with some of the companies that came to campus to recruit.

We scheduled our first conference in conjunction with the State of Illinois Department of Rehabilitation Services, inviting the same companies that sent representatives to other job placement conferences at the University. The number of major companies participating in our conference swelled over the years as word spread about the high-quality job candidates. The conference later moved from a Champaign hotel to what is now the University of Illinois at Springfield, which had many rooms available for interviews and areas for displays and demonstrations. The event grew from a half-day to two days.

Shortly after I started working at the Rehabilitation Center a local radio station called and indicated a desire to prepare a program on rehabilitation. I was quick and to the point. "I can do that." I developed a format that called for me to interview experts in the fields of disability and rehabilitation, and the fifteen-minute program ran for about five years.

I couldn't be director of the Rehabilitation Center because I don't have a doctorate. But when Joe Larsen became ill and died in 1989, the acting dean asked me to take on more responsibilities. They also changed my title from assistant to associate director. I took care of administrative duties that did not involve the academic unit. A lot of the projects I had been working on had to be put on hold as I got involved in a tremendous amount of desk work. Warrick Armstrong, who directed another unit in the college, was named acting director and was terrific. He was kind and gentle when dealing with the division's problems, and kept the staff functioning highly.

In the search for a new division director we found just one candidate with all the qualifications. Paul Leung had a Ph.D., had administered academic programs in rehabilitation and had directed a service program at two other universities. Paul was hired and I served on the search committee. My long-time friend, Brad Hedrick, now serves as the division's director and is doing an outstanding job.

Louise's mother died of lung cancer in 1988. I had always told Emma Fortman that I would write a book and am sorry I failed to finish it before her death.

In 1988 we lost Oscar, the Westie who was almost seventeen. Since Louise and I have had dogs as pets for most of our lives, we again tried to find a replacement as quickly as possible. We located another Westie we named McDougall. He celebrated his fourteenth birthday in November of 2002 and I would describe his health as marginal.

Arthritis had developed meanwhile around the rods in my back. It became difficult and painful, both physically and mentally, to deal with the expanded duties of associate director and the ever-increasing back pain. Reluctantly I told Paul Leung that I would like to work half-time for about six months, using up all my leave and vacation, and take leave Aug. 20 when my contract expired. He agreed and I became a half-time employee during the spring and summer of 1991.

Despite the pain I briefly considered still another job change shortly before leaving the university. In the late winter of 1991 I received a phone call from Mike Jackson, whom I had hired as a booth announcer at Channel 3 while he was still in high school. Jackson eventually took a television position in Chicago, became Midwest correspondent for NBC and was a popular anchor. He had opened his own consulting business before he made that special call to me.

He asked if I would consider applying for the job of director of the Illinois Department of Rehabilitation Services, as it was called then. I said it was an honor to be considered, but my back was not in very good shape and I didn't think I could handle the stress. Mike responded with good arguments, so I finally asked what I would have to do. I sent my resume, underwent a state police background check and was interviewed by Gov. Jim Edgar. I asked Edgar why he wanted me for the job. His reply made me feel older than I was. He said that when he was growing up in Charleston, Ill., he watched me on television. He said I would be a good person to tell people in Illinois about changes he wanted to make in the department.

I did not get the job. A friend who also was close to Edgar told me later that I lost it because of a dispute among Edgar, Chicago Mayor Richard M. Daley and U of I President Stanley Ikenberry about who would be the next chancellor at the University of Illinois at Chicago. As the story goes, Ikenberry prevailed in the dispute, and James Stukel won the chancellor's job. I was told that Daley then called Edgar and said, "You owe me one." That "one" turned out to be a Chicagoan who was named director of the state service agency. I asked Ikenberry about it but he had no comment. Of course Stukel later became president of the University of Illinois. Was I a victim of a political dispute? I will probably never know.

Stanley O. Ikenberry, president emeritus, University of Illinois and former president of the American Council on Education:
"Tom's major contribution to my presidency...was to open my eyes to the superb reputation and rich heritage of the University of Illinois in breaking new ground to open opportunities for higher education to disabled students, young people who in every sense deserved the very best Illinois had to offer...Tom is now a 'professional volunteer,' I am told; but Tom has always been a professional and a volunteer ambassador of the highest quality."

Robert W. Evans, former director of U of I Office of Public Affairs:
"I considered him one of my most valuable staff members...I still consider Tom a close friend and was proud to sponsor him for membership in the Champaign-Urbana Kiwanis Club. Tom has no equal as a professional or gentleman."

Fred Mohn, former head of U of I News Bureau:
"When Tom Jones joined the News Bureau at the University of Illinois, he developed the most successful news operation of any during my fourteen years as bureau manager...No one contributed more to a productive atmosphere...Hiring Tom is one of the smartest decisions I've ever made."

Professor R. W. Armstrong, who worked with Tom in the Division of Rehabilitation Education Services at the U of I:
"Tom perhaps has a special rapport with students with disabilities because of his own disability. But much more significant I think is his personality. He is a kind, considerate and friendly person and it is these qualities that make him such a successful advisor and counselor...In retirement, Tom is deeply involved in volunteering his time and expertise to many individuals and causes, and to sponsoring students with disabilities in scholastic and community endeavors. He is very generous to others with his time and resources."

Paul Leung, former director of the Division of Rehabilitation Education Services at the U of I:
"Tom is tolerant and accepting of new viewpoints and perspectives, even in his personal situation with his back and spinal injury. I know it hasn't been easy and often painful but he continues to persist. I don't think I could have survived my initial year without his knowledge about the Division program and the UI."

Floyd 'Gordie' Gordon, former neighbor and business partner:
"I know of no task that Tom took on that he did not finish. He became a very successful broadcaster, teacher, spokesman, and above all his dedication to the university's rehabilitation program was outstanding. He gave them countless hours of his time and was always willing to help a struggling student. He was forever grateful for what the program did for him and Louise."

12

Advice for the Medical Profession

I thought retirement meant Louise and I could do a lot of traveling. Perhaps we would go back to Florida in December. Maybe we could stay through January and avoid the worst of the central Illinois winter. But Louise was still working. Though she had a month's vacation, she was a key player in developing a new system for university students to register by computer. It was hard for the two of us to go anywhere for long periods of time in the winter, and I didn't want to leave Louise behind. I found myself with a lot of time on my hands.

So I wrote a Champaign radio station to see if they had anything I could do. Mike Haile, the top voice at the station, responded with a "yes" almost instantaneously.

I began hosting an hour-long Sunday morning interview show featuring local, area and national personalities. Most interviews I recorded over the telephone during the week before the show. One of my best was with Jack Brickhouse, the Hall of Fame announcer for the Cubs and Bears. Another favorite interview was with former Marquette University basketball coach Al McGuire.

The show took a lot of time, and after doing it for more than a year I decided I was not having the fun I thought I would have. Today's radio is just not the same as it was when I was a high school DJ in Carbondale. I bowed out to try something else.

Before I left the station in 1993 I was named grand marshal of the Champaign-Urbana Fourth of July parade. A vehicle pulled a cart that carried my chair and me, sitting proudly. I wanted the crowd to see first-hand that a person with a major disability could accomplish enough in life to be rewarded as the grand marshal.

During a Florida trip in 1990 Louise started to have a lot of pain in her left shoulder. In the following four years she became more limited in her ability to transfer from chair to bed, chair to car, etc. The orthopedics department at Carle Hospital in Urbana said they could not do anything except replace her shoulder.

The doctor who was the most logical candidate for surgeon said he had done about three shoulder replacements a year at Carle, but never on a person who used a wheelchair. He had no idea what she would have to go through in terms of rehabilitation after the surgery. I asked for the names of the two best shoulder-replacement surgeons in the country. One was at Mayo Clinic in Rochester, Minn. We made an appointment to see the doctor and learned that Mayo did 300 shoulder replacements a year, most by the same doctor. We knew we wanted him to operate on Louise. We made an appointment for surgery on July 19, 1994. Dr. Robert Cofield took about three hours for the surgery and said Louise should have very good recovery in several months. After surgery, Louise spent two weeks in the Mayo rehabilitation unit, one of the nicest and fanciest rehab units I've ever seen.

At times, however, both Louise and I became frustrated with the doctors and therapists. They had more experience dealing with newly injured young people and elderly stroke victims, but they weren't used to dealing with someone who knew how to be disabled. For example, they were determined to make Louise sit on a cushion, something she had never done in her life. She never needed one. With normal feeling in her body, she is able to change position if she feels uncomfortable.

I am different. Because of my paraplegia, I have used a cushion since I was injured.

But during the first few days at the rehab unit, they reduced Louise to tears with their demand that she sit on a cushion. She tried it, but found it uncomfortable because she was forced to sit at a different height than she was used to. We finally convinced them to give it up.

The doctors and therapists also were concerned about how I could help Louise. I assured them I could help push her chair. They wanted proof. I told them, "I can do it the same way I did when we were in the Mall of America before the surgery. I put my right hand on her left push handle and push my chair with the left hand." I had to demonstrate. I also had to show them how I could assist her in getting into the lift device that would move her from bed to wheelchair. They were impressed and somewhat amazed.

They never had seen a married couple, both in wheelchairs, so independent. We knew how to be disabled. We just needed instruction on how to rehabilitate a new shoulder. I hope our three-week experience there made it easier for the next person in a similar situation.

We rented a hospital-type bed and put it in the family room where Louise had a good view of the back yard and the TV set. We had a health-care agency provide help to her in getting out of bed in the morning, going to bed at night, bathing and other personal care. I seldom ventured farther from home than the grocery store. If Louise had to go to the bathroom during the day, I helped her with the urinal. Our system worked quite well for three months.

Then we went back to the doctor at Mayo, who wanted to make sure she was strong enough to return to work. Dr. Cofield gave his approval, but recommended that Louise work only half time for a few months. She did for one week, then resumed working eight hours a day.

As I talked with my brother after Louise's surgery to give him good news, he expressed concern about Sarah, his wife of more than 40 years. She just wasn't herself. She felt she was losing her mind. Then she began having fainting spells. She was sent to Jewish Hospital in St. Louis for brain tests. The report was devastating. The preliminary report was that Sarah might have the human equivalent of Mad Cow Disease, Creutzfeld-Jakob Disease. She had not been to Great Britain, but somewhere may have eaten imported beef that was tainted. She died almost exactly one year after the symptoms first appeared. The family still wonders how Sarah contracted this dreadful disease, if indeed that is what it was. Medical specialists report there are about 300 cases of piron diseases in the United States each year and Creutzfeld-Jakob is one of them.

We made two trips to Carbondale in two weeks. The first was for Sarah's funeral. The second was for a happier occasion, my high school's fortieth class reunion. The reunion was wonderful. I'd missed an earlier one because I was fishing in Canada, and didn't think I'd enjoy a reunion anyway. Was I wrong! As part of the program each attendee gave a short talk about life since high school. It is always a problem giving an ex-broadcaster a microphone with no time limit. Seeing all the old friends made me emotional, and I told the class of my love for its members. There I was in 1951, the only one in a wheelchair, and the class treated me like everybody else. I told my old classmates they were one of the reasons I was able to become an active, responsible human being. After the dinner one of the toughest guys in the class told me, "I never thought I would come to a high school reunion and cry." I returned to my forty-fifth reunion as master of ceremonies.

I was invited to join the Champaign-Urbana Kiwanis Club. Since I had extra time, I thought the Kiwanis would make good use of it. Ours is a hard-working club, mainly providing service to children. In fact, Young Children, Priority One is the slogan of Kiwanis International. Our club has sponsored Little League baseball for over fifty years and we have almost 1,500 young people playing baseball every year.

I have served on several committees and am chairman of the Tom Jones Challenger League Committee. This league permits children with physical and mental disabilities to play baseball. We modify the rules a bit. If a player can only hit off a tee, that's what he or she does. Every player bats every inning and nobody ever strikes out. We try to pair each child with an able-bodied buddy to assist where necessary.

This league came about because I filled in at our Little League baseball honors banquet in 1998 when the scheduled speaker cancelled because of bad weather. I spoke with no preparation to 500 children and adults about why I was in the wheelchair, about playing baseball in a wheelchair and about my life as a television sports reporter. Sometimes I believe you can deliver better speeches without much preparation. The impact of the speech gave our club the idea of starting a baseball league for youngsters with disabilities and naming it after me. It is a terrific honor. I would hope others who read about this league will consider starting a Challenger League in their community. It is an official program of Little League International and they can give you all the details.

In the spring of 1999 another event interfered with the more relaxed lifestyle I had hoped for. The man who wrote the foreword for this book established with the U of I College of Communications the Roger Ebert Overlooked Film Festival. It features films that Ebert, the Pulitzer Prize winner who graduated from the U of I, believes are outstanding, but have had little exposure.

One film Ebert selected for the first festival was from Australia and told the story of a young woman named Heather Rose who suffered from cerebral palsy and was mistreated by a caregiver. The film, 'Dance Me to My Song,' brought Heather, who wrote and starred in the film, to Champaign to take part in the festival. When Ebert and the college could not find anyone to help with Heather, Louise and I volunteered to host her. We found lodging for her and her current caregiver, equipped it with the foods she could eat and drove her and her power wheelchair around in our lift-equipped van.

Rick Kaplan, then president of CNN USA, asked Louise and me in 1999 to appear in a promotional spot that ran several times on the network. Friends as far away as California saw it.

I still had a lot of time on my hands and wanted to expand my volunteer work. I did that when I was asked to join the advisory board of Champaign-Urbana Special Recreation Department. It provides services to people with disabilities through the Champaign and Urbana Park Districts. I narrated a videotape that was entered in a national competition to choose the best special recreation department in the country, based on size of the population served. We won the gold medal.

I also began on a more regular basis to read for blind and visually impaired students. Until recently, I continued volunteering for the Developmental Services Center, serving on one of the boards.

The first Mary Lois Jones Hays Outstanding Student Health Programs Employee Award was given in the spring of 2000. Louise and I, my brother and other family members contribute to the Southern Illinois University Foundation, so the award will continue indefinitely. For the past 30 years Louise and I have developed a fund in the Division of Rehabilitation Education Services at the University of Illinois which benefits current students with disabilities.

In 1996 I was nominated and elected to the Illinois Basketball Coaches Association Hall of Fame Media Division. Lee Cabutti, whom I met when he coached in Herrin, nominated me. The Hall of Fame banquet draws more than 1,000 people each spring to Illinois State University in Normal.

Louise finally decided to retire at the end of May in 1997. I had begged her to do that for several years, but she had not been ready. She was a popular and happy U of I employee for thirty-five years.

Now we were both free to see the world. But traveling became more of a problem because of advancing infirmities. Pain in my own shoulders and back was increasing. We were pretty much confined to visiting family and taking day trips to Chicago area shopping centers. Despite cutting back on travel, we stayed busy.

The fiftieth anniversary of the Division of Rehabilitation Education Services approached, and Louise and I were involved in the planning. Several other alumni produced a history of the division, and I chose most of the photos. We made the April, 1998, celebration a big one because the division had been a godsend to Louise, so many other students and me. This was the first program to offer a complete college education for students with severe physical disabilities. It allowed us to be competitive in the workplace and now enjoy a high standard of living in retirement. It was successful because of the innovation, desire and drive of Tim Nugent, and because of the students who were helped by it.

For several months I had experienced severe pain in my left shoulder. After the anniversary celebration, I underwent surgery to repair a torn rotator cuff on May 6, 1998. Dr. Robert Gurtler at Carle Hospital told me the injury was so severe he did not know how I could have used the arm for the six previous months. Apparently, the rotator cuff simply wore out because of the strain put on it during sixty years of using a wheelchair.

Because of the HMO limit on my time in the hospital following surgery, I was home the next day, though my surgeon and another doctor recommended I remain in the hospital several days. I began going downhill, and on the third day threw up blood. I was bleeding internally. The next morning, I lost consciousness and was returned by ambulance to the same hospital I had left four days earlier. Tests showed I had several bleeding ulcers, stress ulcers. I believe if HMOs don't change the way they deal with patients, this country is going to allow some lawsuits against them. My insurer paid dearly for having me sent home too early. It cost them $6,000 to take me back into the hospital and give me three units of blood. I paid nothing.

Apparently I am a fast healer, because it took me only five weeks after my shoulder surgery to be able to lift my weight and to do transfers with the repaired arm and shoulder. But until then I received the same kind of assistance provided Louise after her shoulder replacement and to me in 1983 after back surgery. Health-care workers came to our home morning and night. I lost all my modesty, but was given no other choice. The most difficult part was to surrender my independence.

Before writing what I am about to write, irritating many of my good friends who are doctors, I am alive today due to the expertise and skills of members of the medical profession. Could I be in better shape if other decisions had been made? Perhaps. I have always been an active participant in discussions with my doctors and believe that my input has added to their knowledge as they deal with my problems.

However, this brings me to a subject that has concerned me for many years. I really don't believe many physicians know how to deal with a person who has had a long-term disability and who then develops one or more of the infirmities of old age. Doctors tell me that not much in this area is taught in medical school. They deal with people who are ill. They deal with people who need surgery. But the medical profession at many times is at a loss to what to do for a person who has a long-term, major disability, and then develops another problem created by the aging process. Some physiatrists deal primarily with persons who have disabilities, but the few dealings I have had with them have been less than satisfactory. I have no suggestions about how to solve this problem. Perhaps medical schools could do a better job of teaching future physicians how to deal with persons who have long-term disabilities. Complicating the situation even farther are the demands placed on physicians by insurance companies which limit certain tests and the amount of time a doctor can visit with his patient.

Harold D. Guither, president of the Kiwanis Club of Champaign-Urbana in 1993 when Tom joined:
"I saw Tom as one of the most dedicated board members...Tom showed a special initiative in getting the little league for handicapped youngsters under way...Tom had a very unfortunate accident early in his life, but he has not let that prevent him from moving ahead with his education and carving out a useful career here at the University of Illinois and serving his community through Kiwanis and other groups."

Robert F. Toalson, former general manager, Champaign Park District:
"What impresses me about Tom is his sense of commitment. Once he takes on a project, you can count on him getting the job done and done well."

"Dale Morrissey, CEO, Developmental Services Center, Champaign:
"Tom has spent countless hours advocating for supports and services which enable people with physical and developmental disabilities to live more fulfilling and productive lives."

13

Negotiation, Not More Laws

Let's talk about some more practicalities involved in living with a disability. Over all, expenses are higher and more numerous. Louise and I have affordable medical insurance. We are lucky. For some kinds of disability, I know this is hard to come by. One should find proper advice about federal and state income taxes. I believe people with disabilities may have federal benefits available that the government doesn't readily advertise. For instance, when we were working, mileage to and from work came right off the top of our taxes, and it required a lot of digging to find out that was legal.

We worked steadily from early adulthood until our retirements. However, some people with disabilities think the world owes them a living. It doesn't. Nobody owes you anything. I understand that if you're in an accident that was someone else's fault, you should expect to receive compensation. I'm talking about someone whose disability is no one's fault. It rankles me to see people with disabilities chaining themselves together and sitting in front of a bus to make a point. It gives the able-bodied population, the power base in the country, a negative feeling toward people with disabilities. How many positives have come from such demonstrations? Very few.

Please don't get me wrong. It is not right for you to be excluded from a job because you have a disability. I don't agree that persons with disabilities should blindly accept situations that are dictated by others. I just believe there is a better way to bring attention to the problems. I have always found it is much better to discuss calmly with the power structure whatever problem you perceive than it is to mount an ugly and ineffective public protest. I've had repeated success talking with lawmakers and corporate officials. Negotiating takes longer, but has a more positive and permanent effect. Yes, it is true, you can get more with honey than with vinegar.

I tell my black friends when they remind me that thirty years ago they had to sit at the back of the bus that in those years I couldn't even get on the bus. Certainly a much different kind of discrimination, but discrimination nonetheless. You can't expect the world suddenly to become totally accessible or for society to suddenly change attitudes toward your situation. Change takes time.

    I see a lot of positive results from the Americans with Disabilities Act. But it is not working wonders. The language within the law is so vague that it will be years and years before the courts can figure out what it means and whom it protects. If you read the ADA closely, you will see that it is not very specific in terms of what it is supposed to do and who determines when the law is violated. Large amounts of money will have to be spent before judges and juries can decide just what ADA means. I have read that at least 800 different disabilities have been identified. Those include obesity, alcoholism and drug addiction. Even airline personnel who have to wear glasses have asked for protection under ADA. I read recently that, despite ADA, fewer people with disabilities are working today than when the law was passed.

    In terms of employment, if six people of equal skill apply for a job and one has a disability, that person may not be treated equally. If the interviewer has never associated with people who have disabilities, most likely that interviewer will not know how to deal with this unknown quantity. You must be better than other job applicants just to get past the initial interview. If you are better and if you can convince the interviewer that you are, which is not easy, you will have a fair chance of getting the job. Even for those who are not disabled, it's a very competitive world. Do all you can to be prepared. Read all you can about the business that is interviewing you. Be ready to tell the interviewer how you can help the company with the skills you have acquired.

    And look as good as you can. I understand that many physical deformities are beyond anyone's control and are part of how you look. However, though you may not have much money, it doesn't take much effort to have a clean body and wear clean clothes. This is part of making a good impression at that interview and it just takes some dedication.

    Transportation is an essential expense, and it does not come cheap. When I buy a motor vehicle, hand controls cost at least an additional $600. The vehicle also must have an automatic transmission. Our first van cost $25,000, plus $18,000 to be retrofitted with a dropped floor and a ramp. As cars were built smaller, we had difficulty pulling our wheelchairs into the space in the back seat, which forced us to purchase larger, more expensive vehicles, the last being a 1991 Cadillac. When Louise stopped driving due to shoulder pain, we switched to vans in 1992 and just recently bought our fourth specially equipped Dodge Caravan.

For many years, most insurance companies charged more than the going rate for drivers who used hand controls. Fortunately, that seems to have changed. But we buy an extra $2 million umbrella policy in case we are in an accident and the other driver decides to sue just because we drove with hand controls.

Pumping gasoline is hard for some people with disabilities. I have enough arm strength to pump my own gasoline, but many times I cannot reach the high slot that takes the credit card. Also, it is unthinking discrimination to convert so many full-serve gasoline stations to self-serve. I understand the financial need that brought this about, but in many ways it takes away the independence of persons with disabilities who drive. This began a project in the fall of 1997 when Illinois State Rep. Tim Johnson asked if I had any ideas regarding how to solve the pump-accessibility problem. I gave him several I thought would work without requiring another law. We have too many laws as it is. The next year Johnson set up a meeting with members of the Illinois Petroleum Marketers Association, Illinois advocacy groups for people with disabilities and me. At first, the industry people pleaded ignorance, saying they had never been told there was a problem. We made them realize there was indeed a problem and that it would worsen as the population grew older. The state lawmaker said he would draft a bill if a solution were not reached in one year.

In the summer of 1999 groups representing people with disabilities, the industry and the Illinois Department of Human Services came to an agreement. Participating stations agreed to pump gasoline and charge self-service prices to individuals with disabilities and qualifying seniors. Accessibility symbols were posted on the signs of participating stations along the interstates. It's another example of what can be done when you talk to the right people in the right way.

Time is valuable, and people with disabilities must spend extra time doing things able-bodied people take for granted. Friends and co-workers don't always understand why it might take me a little longer in a bathroom because of self-catherization. They don't know how much I plan when I go somewhere new for a vacation or a meeting. I have to find out where the bathroom is and how accessible it is to a person in a wheelchair. Rarely—but it has happened—I might have a bowel accident while out in public. That's something constantly on my mind. So, I always make plans, just in case. I leave early for almost everything. It drives Louise crazy, though she accommodates me.

Finding a place to park is another time-consumer, although I got by for more than thirty years without special parking spaces for persons with disabilities. I always found a space and always did quite well. Some with disabilities can't walk very far or have trouble pushing their wheelchairs. I understand that they do need close-up spaces. But the abuse! I have been told that Illinois provides more than 500,000 handicapped parking tags authorized by doctors. Do 500,000 people really need those spaces?

Then there are the other annoyances. For example, when the U of I Assembly Hall was built more than thirty years ago, it was one of the finest places for persons in wheelchairs to watch an event. Due to an aging population it is now one of the many sports stadiums without enough seating for those in wheelchairs or those who have difficulty climbing steps. In New York, a disability rights group sued because the wheelchair seats in Yankee Stadium don't allow them to see the whole field.

Another uncomfortable situation occurs at cocktail parties where most people are standing. It's hard to converse if you are seated. I can think of only two or three people at these kinds of events who had the courtesy to squat or sit while they were talking seriously with me. I have stopped attending cocktail parties and sporting events where accessibility is difficult. Part of the reason is that my life is slower now. But the whole world even today is not accessible to people in wheelchairs. It never will be. And I'm not advocating that it should be.

A positive development is the growing numbers of ramps and curb cuts. I am proud of the fact that I have been successful in convincing numerous businesses to install them. I lost one fight with a clothing store owner who moved into a historic building with inaccessible steps. I was particularly incensed because the store received a government subsidy—part of it my tax money—to make the move. The store has gone out of business. Perhaps a ramp would have made it successful.

Beer truck drivers owe me their thanks for changes at another location. I persuaded the owners to install a ramp from the parking lot to the store. The owner told me the deliverymen think he is terrific as they use the ramp more than anyone else. Perhaps they will name it the Tom Jones Memorial Liquor Store Ramp some day. Curb cuts can cost several hundred dollars apiece, but slopes between sidewalks and streets benefit women pushing baby buggies, Parkinson's disease patients and even bicyclists and skaters in addition to wheelchair users. If you offer a service to people in wheelchairs you also benefit the elderly, the arthritic and others who for some reason may not walk very well.

Another great help is the growing number of easily accessible buses, trains and planes. Champaign-Urbana was, if not the first, one of the first communities in the country with a pilot program putting lifts on buses that run regular routes. Cities provide lifts on all of their buses now. If my car won't start and I can't get a cab, I can wheel down the block and catch a bus.

Embarrassments are another tax on people with disabilities. The way some able-bodied people deal with those with disabilities has disturbed me for years. For example, some experiences in restaurants have made me feel inferior. The waiter would ask my able-bodied companion what I wanted to eat. It was as if he or she did not believe I could read, see or talk just because I was sitting in a wheelchair. The worst instance was when I was in my twenties and visiting Carbondale. I had joined my father in a popular restaurant, and in more than one hour, we were served only water and crackers. The owner finally suggested that we leave, fearing my presence would drive away other customers who thought they might catch something from me. We left without eating and never went back. Many times in a restaurant, grocery store, theater or other public place I've felt that the able-bodied in charge were not comfortable with my presence. It rarely occurs today, but still does. You can learn a lot about how a person feels toward you from their body language.

My favorite grocery store provides a delicatessen counter too high for the employees to see me sitting in my wheelchair. It is embarrassing to have to yell to them. It is not intentional discrimination, but it is unthinking discrimination. I've tried for years to get them to provide a bell so I could attract their attention without shouting. Perhaps someday they will. It almost appears that some in the able-bodied population feel that if you have a disability, you also are dumb.

Other big positives are friends. Good friends. Great friends. Paul Luedtke, his wife and children are some of our best friends. Paul thinks so much of his friends who have disabilities that he has eliminated the front stoop on his house and installed a ramp to his front door.

I am in a wheelchair and there is absolutely nothing I can do about it. On the other hand, if someone constantly referred to me as that guy in a wheelchair, I would be offended. I would hope I have been able to convince friends and co-workers over the years that a wheelchair is just a mode of transportation and has nothing at all to do with my ability to function.

I know some will say Louise and I have been able to enjoy many of our conveniences because we have made a good living at our jobs. This is true. However, if a person with a disability wants to succeed and live a happy, productive life, it can be done without a large sum of money. However, it does require a desire to overcome the difficulties the disability brings and the determination to be a useful member of society.

14

Advocate for the Health of It

There's an old saying in broadcast: tell the story, repeat it, then tell it again. That way you will be sure to be understood.

Let me repeat myself now because I want you to understand that this is of utmost importance. If you are a person with a long-term disability you must be your own advocate. To be successful as an advocate you must have a doctor who is willing to listen to what you have to say. The medical profession must be willing to learn from you, the patient. This is a vitally important lesson for anybody with a disability. You must be your own advocate in medical situations whether you are dealing with a nurse, a doctor, a physical therapist or whatever. If you've lived with your problem long enough, you know your situation better than they will ever know it.

One advantage I've had over the years is that I'm a pretty good talker. Most of the time I can produce a convincing argument that backs up my point of view. I have been able to make the doctors I've dealt with understand that I know my situation at least just as well as they do. I've lived with this disability for sixty years and I know how my body works. If I believe a certain test or x-ray will diagnose what is bothering me, I will ask my doctor to prescribe it. Usually, he or she will.

Every one of us, whether we have a disability or not, will develop some physical problem as we get older, whether it's arthritis, an eye problem, loss of hearing, difficulty in walking, whatever. And if you suffer a long-term disability on top of the new ailment, you and your medical provider must figure out how much of the new problem is caused by aging and how much of the new problem is caused or amplified by the original disability. I understand it may be tough to persuade your medical provider that you know at least as much about the situation as he or she does. But for your own sake you have to try.

I am fortunate to have as my primary care physician Dr. Eugene Greenberg, who has been associated with Carle Clinic in Urbana for many years. The man listens to me. I would guess he is thinking about retirement, and that concerns me a great deal. At my age, I don't look forward to breaking in a new doctor.

Don't be intimidated by a doctor. Ask questions—the right ones. Go to an appointment with a list of everything you want explained and everything you want to explain. Don't accept everything the doctor says as gospel. Demand enough time for the appointment. Be a good listener as well as a good talker. Communicate. Evaluate.

Of course, a more recent problem involves how many tests and how much medication your insurance provider is willing to let you have.

I believe many young people with disabilities harm themselves by trying to be overachievers, especially those who use wheelchairs as their main mode of transportation. What harm are they doing to their arms and shoulders by practicing and racing super-long distances? What will happen when their joints are in such bad shape that they can't move themselves into a chair or lift themselves in and out of bed? Persons with disabilities now live as long as everyone else. Their first responsibility is to maintain good health so that those later years will be good ones. But when they are young, they want to prove they can do as many physically taxing events as everyone else. People with disabilities are just like everyone else at a young age. They think they are invincible.

Many of my good friends will disagree with me on this, saying they now have proper training sessions that will prevent these joint breakdowns from occurring. I hope they are right and I am wrong. Only time will tell.

I also recommend that persons who have a disability try to avoid stress as much as they can. Most of the stress in my life has been psychological rather than physical, though it sometimes surfaces in urinary tract infections. I wear my stress on my sleeve. It's always out there. Louise, if she is stressed, hides it better than I. Hers is caused by outside things. Mine is more self-induced. I am very critical of myself. In many cases I relieve it by saying a nasty word or yelling, and if I get a stiff neck, I know it's because I'm really stressed out. That is a very visible way I know when my stress levels are harming my system. I am told stress can cause problems in our weakest body parts. Perhaps that is why my back gives me so much trouble. I am a worrier and I inherited those genes from my father, who was one of the world's worst worriers.

The age at which you are injured and the severity of the injury make a difference in your outlook. If you're young, as I was, the psychological impact is easier to overcome. You have very little recollection of what it was like to walk and do things that people do when they walk. If you are in your teens, as in most of the cases of spinal cord injuries, it is much more devastating.

A major problem, one I don't know how to solve, is how to hammer into the brains of injured people how they must take care of themselves. How do they learn to take care of thinning skin and bladder infections? How do they learn to dress themselves? Where do they learn to protect themselves if they fall? How do they learn what kind of wheelchair and cushion is best for them? Obviously, physicians and therapists play a big part in a person's rehabilitation. However, unless an injured youngster has loving, dedicated parents or other care givers who will go to the ends of the earth to find out how their son, daughter or charge needs to be able to survive this drastic lifestyle change, such an injury can be life-threatening.

I have known several persons who, beyond the immediate physical impact, became alcoholics or drug addicts because they never learned to take care of themselves and decided being spaced out was the easiest way to deal with their problems.

I really do hate to say I am not 'normal.' I'm not normal compared with people who walk. I'm different, but I'm also different in that I'm white-skinned in comparison with people who have black skin. I'm a Type A personality, compared with people who are more laid-back. I'm a time freak, in contrast to people who can be thirty minutes late and not be bothered by it. Everybody is unique, different from others in so many, many ways.

In today's politically correct world, people invent as many ways as possible to refer to others. I think the words 'handicapped' and 'disabled' are acceptable. I am, however, a person with a disability, and I emphasize 'person' first. I am not a disabled person. You wouldn't say 'non-disabled person.' A local clinic raised a sign that said 'parking for disabled persons.' It should say 'parking for people with disabilities.' Many businesses do this.

My disability prevents me from walking. That creates a handicap when I arrive at a place where people need to walk or climb steps. My disability is caused by paraplegia. Some people want to be called 'physically challenged.' All of us are physically challenged, whether or not we have an identifiable disability. When I was first injured I was 'crippled.' That was the accepted word for people who could not walk. When I was no longer crippled I was 'handicapped.' Then I became 'disabled.' Since disability rights groups and action groups got involved, I don't really know what I should be called. Some say I should be termed 'able disabled.' Perhaps I am 'handicappable.' I'm not sure. We could produce a whole list of names, most of which make me want to throw up.

A lot of younger people with disabilities want different terms. Most of us who are older don't really care what we are called. Unless the term is intentionally discriminatory, let's not make a big deal about what people with disabilities should be called.

I have waged a so-far unsuccessful campaign on two words. The media still doesn't seem to have learned that people who use wheelchairs are not 'confined' to wheelchairs. Wheelchair 'bound' is similar. 'Wheelchair user' is correct. Obviously, we leave that wheelchair to go to bed, take showers and so on. Maybe some day my colleagues in the media will catch on.

15

It Takes a Sense of Humor

I am a perfectionist. I've never done one thing with which I was totally satisfied. Not one interview. Not one term paper. Not one project. And I lose my temper at the stupid things I do.

I truly believe the critical self-analysis is good because I always have something to reach for. Perhaps I fear that if I were ever to do something that I felt totally satisfied about, my life would be over. What else would be out there to try for? If we ever found the end of the universe, what else would there be?

I've been able to build my own power base in Champaign-Urbana, making my situation in terms of being a person with a disability different from a lot of others. I have been very lucky to be a person who many people recognize because of all my years on television and in the university system. I worked hard to put myself in that position. I could go to a businessman who didn't have a ramp at his store and ask him put one in. I can't tell you how many times I did that, and those ramps are located all over Champaign and Urbana. Anyone with a disability who is reading this can do the same things I have done. Make yourself known to the power structure in your community. Gain its trust.

The Champaign-Urbana News-Gazette recently printed a feature commemorating its 150th anniversary. It featured what they called 'Good Sports', and I was fortunate to be included. The writer asked me how I would describe a good sport, and I replied, "Someone who plays by the rules." You may not like the rules, but you must play by them no matter where you encounter them. Certainly, you can work to change the rules in an orderly fashion, but don't thumb your nose at them just because they make life inconvenient for you.

Louise wants more humor in this book. I have fun in most everything I do. There is plenty of humor in dealing with a disability. However, it's not always obvious. I've basically been an old man since I was shot at age six. But I do have a sense of humor.

When the St. Louis Cardinals won the pennant and the World Series we threw a party to celebrate. I still have that child-size Cardinal uniform my dad bought me. So the last time St. Louis won the World Series we stuffed the uniform. We made a balloon head and put a Cardinal cap on top. We set the dummy in a chair. It frustrated our dog, Oscar, no end because the dummy would not pet him.

I rented a male belly dancer for Louise's fiftieth birthday party. When I turned fifty she rented a billboard on a main Champaign street. During one of our first dates, Louise told me she remembered Dave Garroway doing a radio show in Chicago. I remembered him as an early host of the Today Show on TV. So, I remarked, "How old are you anyway." The billboard she rented showed my picture with the words, "How old are you anyway."

I also have a lot of fun with my 1948 Wurlitzer jukebox, three plays for a quarter. It was the last bubble-top machine Wurlitzer made for seventy-eight rpm records. Louise and I love the big band music of the thirties and forties, such as Glenn Miller's, and vocalists from the next two decades, including Frank Sinatra. I also like some of Elvis Presley's songs and country music. Willie Nelson is one of our favorites. Louise enjoys some classical music, but I don't understand it.

The Wurlitzer is an old man's toy, along with my nickel slot machine that was made in 1937, the same year I was made. I have the best of both worlds. I own the machine and I own the money. Otherwise, I'm not a gambler other than placing an occasional dollar bet with a friend on some sporting event.

When I was young being a Cardinal fan was almost like a religion. It was something I lived and breathed. I could tell you the names of all the players, their batting averages, pitchers' records and so on. I lost a lot of heart during the baseball strike. For about three years I refused to buy a ticket and go to a game.

I believe professional baseball needs salary caps, just like pro football and basketball. TV reporting jaded my attitude about sports—particularly college sports. As I talked with coaches and players and saw what was happening, I became discouraged about the health of amateur sports. I spent increasing amounts of time on my sports programs talking about players in trouble with the law, players who weren't keeping their grades up, players with bad attitudes and coaches always on the lookout for better jobs. Amateur sports at the college level was more professional than the average fan assumed. That made sports reporting less fun and it made me less enthusiastic as a fan.

Family and friends become more important as we age. All too often younger family members forget how important it is to maintain good relationships with those who love you. Louise and I continue to enjoy visits with my brother, his daughters Laura and Mary and their families and with Louise's sister Mary and her husband. We cherish Thanksgiving and Christmas dinners with the Dahnckes and Luedtkes, a tradition the families have enjoyed for almost thirty years.

I have been fairly healthy. I have a wonderful education. I was gainfully employed for as long as I wanted to be. I met a wonderful woman and we've had more than forty years of happy marriage. What else could I have wanted?

I don't have many regrets. For the most part I've been able to work in a profession I enjoyed and for which I was fairly well prepared. About the only regret in terms of my broadcast career was that I very much wanted to be a Major League baseball announcer. I never got there. When I might have been following in the footsteps of Harry Caray or Jack Brickhouse, the inaccessibility of most of the older baseball stadiums would have made that dream almost impossible even if I had the ability. Many newer stadiums have elevators to the broadcast booth. But time has passed me by.

What would I have done differently in my life? I never would have been shot. But I do believe I am a much better person for having a disability than I would have been otherwise. It has been a good life. I certainly am glad I married Louise. We still respect each other and enjoy each other's company. Of course, we get angry with each other, but we work it through. We give each other space but make major decisions together. Louise and I celebrated our fortieth wedding anniversary on Aug. 15, 1999, by inviting eighteen of our closest friends and family members to a dinner at an Urbana restaurant to thank them for their love and support for all the years we have been married.

What comes next? Staying busy. Staying useful. I read at least three newspapers a day. Occasionally I will read a sports book. I don't enjoy reading as much as Louise does. She subscribes to several book clubs and is skilled at crossword puzzles. I don't have a large enough vocabulary for that.

Though we follow politics, neither Louise nor I belong to a political party. We tend to vote for the person instead of the party affiliation. I would describe myself as a financial conservative and a social liberal. Our basic values and how we want the world to be are about the same, but Louise doesn't like to discuss politics with me. That's because I have a habit of taking the other side, no matter what she says.

Though I am not religious, I say Godspeed to all the people who are working on how to fix the damaged nerve in the spinal column, attempting to make it rejuvenate. When or if they learn how to do that, I believe it would not help many people who were injured long ago. Too many other things have happened in the body, like deterioration of the muscles. However, 10,000 or so people in this country suffer a spinal cord injury each year. Perhaps those people with newer injuries will benefit. I would not.

I recently visited Dr. John McDonald's stem cell research lab at Washington University in St. Louis. It is too bad that the controversy surrounding the use of stem cells in research has delayed their possible use in efforts to help find cures for disease and help those with spinal cord injuries. I do believe Dr. McDonald and his research associates are on the verge of finding some answers that will make life better for many people who are now suffering debilitating injury or disease.

Living next door to us in Carbondale in those early days after my injury was a Pentecostal minister, Sister Pearl. She wanted my parents to take me to one of her tent meetings for hands-on healing. Fortunately, common sense prevailed and I never did experience hands-on healing.

I was baptized into the First Christian Church of Carbondale, but my family drifted away from the church. Louise and I were married in a Catholic Church, the religion she practices, though she no longer attends regularly.

I believe I am a moral person. I have a moral code. I know right from wrong and try to practice that code every day. I had, and still do have, a plan for my life. People tell me God also has a plan. Some believe He is in control of everything that happens in the universe. I've actually had people tell me I was shot for a reason: "You are God's messenger on this earth to show what can be done after a hardship."

That's a crock. When I was younger, I would ask myself if we are controlled by a loving God, why would he allow a six-year-old—whose main failing in life was to pick tulips from a neighbor's yard—to be shot down and turned into a paraplegic? Why wouldn't he pick an adult who robbed a couple of stores or killed somebody? However, as I matured, I no longer asked that question. I know now we have free will. My free will as a six-year-old was to take the longer road to Mr. Marvin's store.

Tom Jones' brother, Carl Jones Jr.:
"After his injury, naturally his life changed. But with his wonderful father and mother, Tom embarked on a life-changing pursuit of what he has achieved—a well-rounded and completely adjusted adult. Tom is a person who has given and is still giving to a society that, I believe, for the most part appreciates and marvels at what he has been able to achieve."

About the Author

Tom Jones has used a wheelchair for sixty of his sixty-six years after being shot in the back in 1943. He earned two degrees from the University of Illinois and his careers ranged from commercial television to public relations to rehabilitation services. He has been married to the same woman for forty-four years.

0-595-27166-9

Printed in the United States
39267LVS00002B/154-201